Praise for Saul Frampton's

WHEN I AM PLAYING WITH MY CAT, HOW DO I KNOW THAT SHE IS NOT PLAYING WITH ME?

"Although they were first published more than four centuries ago, Montaigne's essays can seem as topical as the morning newspaper. As more than one admirer has discovered, Montaigne's essential gift—the art of conversation rendered on the page—is a timeless one."

—*The Christian Science Monitor*

"Montaigne's essays delight in human sensuality, uniqueness, even unpredictability. Though [his] early essays were about war, the later essays are playful, uninhibited, and in parts painfully intimate (sexual dysfunction, the passing of kidney stones, etc.). Frampton, in his lighthearted book, explores the shift in Montaigne's thinking. . . . [He] shows how Montaigne's later essays are full of fascination and observation and how he approaches practical issues—his health, his political obligations, his role as a winemaker—with an enviable equanimity."

—*Los Angeles Times*

"Frampton offers a celebration of perhaps the most enjoyable and yet profound of all Renaissance writers, whose essays went on to have a huge impact on figures as diverse as Shakespeare, Emerson and Orson Welles, and whose thoughts, even today, offer a guide and unprecedented insight into the simple matter of being alive."

—*The Washington Times*

"Scholarly, but not pedantic, this is a book to be savored over time. As with Montaigne's essays, it is one which can be opened and read at any point without interrupting its flow. . . . Frampton's extensive knowledge of literary history is evident."
—*The Post and Courier*

"With deceptive casualness, Frampton renders a rigorous history of ideas in this engaging account of the life and the work of Michel de Montaigne. . . . His extraordinary achievement is in conveying—and inviting the reader to commune with—Montaigne's unique sensibility and his take on death, sex, travel, friendship, kidney stones, the human thumb, and above all, 'the power of the ordinary and the unremarkable, the value of the here-and-now.' . . . This scholarly romp through the Renaissance is a jewel."
—*Publishers Weekly* (starred review)

"The skeptical and humane French nobleman has always had his admirers, and Frampton's learned, subtle, and engaging book shows why."
—*Maclean's*

"Ingenious. . . . Passionately written and full to bursting with digressions and anecdotes, Frampton's book does an excellent job of bringing Montaigne and his historical context to life. It is this vivid evocation of the time that emerges as the book's greatest strength. We see how the philosopher's celebration of daily life . . . went against not only the dominant philosophical currents of the day but also the violent upheavals of 16th-century France. What comes through the strongest is an inspiring sense of the philosopher's remarkable independence of thought and enduring relevance."
—*The Sunday Times* (London)

"In Montaigne's intense self-absorption, Frampton discerns the rich literary fruit of a stunning midlife volte-face. . . . Recognizing the twenty-first century's own need for advocates of life-affirming tolerance, readers will embrace this insightful portrait." —*Booklist* (starred review)

"One of the best books I have read on Montaigne. . . . Frampton argues that to read Montaigne is 'to touch base with oneself' and to learn how to act within our capacities, to accept and even to savour them. . . . He demonstrates that the more Montaigne observed ordinary life, the more remarkable he found it, and the more he felt impelled to plunge back into its mess. . . . Four centuries on, Montaigne still speaks to us." —Nicholas Shakespeare, *The Daily Telegraph* (London)

"Frampton's book stands as a work in its own right and should encourage anyone unfamiliar with Montaigne to read the original." —*The Oxford Times*

"*When I Am Playing With My Cat* sends us back to the *Essays* with both a deepened understanding and a deepened appreciation of the work of this real-life man for all seasons." —*The Washington Independent Review of Books*

Saul Frampton

WHEN I AM PLAYING WITH MY CAT, HOW DO I KNOW THAT SHE IS NOT PLAYING WITH ME?

Saul Frampton studied English and philosophy at the University of East Anglia, wrote a doctorate on Renaissance literature at Oxford, and was a research fellow at Cambridge. He lives in Hove on the Sussex coast.

WHEN I AM PLAYING WITH MY CAT, HOW DO I
KNOW SHE IS NOT PLAYING WITH ME?

When I Am Playing with My Cat, How Do I Know She Is Not Playing with Me?

Montaigne and Being in Touch with Life

SAUL FRAMPTON

Vintage Books
A Division of Random House, Inc.
New York

We are each of us richer than we think . . .

Contents

Preface

Sometime towards the end of the sixteenth century, Michel Eyquem, Seigneur de Montaigne, reached up to the ceiling of his library and scratched off an inscription he had placed there some years before. His library was on the third floor of a round tower standing on a corner of the noble house of Montaigne in Périgord. From his windows he could see into his garden, his courtyard, his vineyards, and into most parts of his house. The house stood on a hill a few miles north of the Dordogne, some thirty miles east of Bordeaux.

Circling Montaigne were his books, a thousand of them, arranged on five shelves on all sides. Through them he leafed 'without order, without plan', getting up from his chair to stroll around the room, sixteen paces in diameter, giving him a circular walk of about fifty paces in circumference. Above his head, classical and biblical quotations curled across the joists and beams of his ceiling, like vines round the branches of a tree.

The inscription Montaigne erased was a line from the Roman poet Lucretius: *Nec nova vivendo procuditur ulla voluptas* – There is no new pleasure to be gained by living longer. It was a sentiment he had previously held dear to. Like most thinkers of his time, Montaigne followed a Christian and a Stoic philosophy, where life was seen as preparation for the afterlife and the task of philosophy was to harden oneself against the vicissitudes of fortune. And of misfortune, Montaigne had experience at close hand. His first-born daughter had died at the age of only two months (the first of five to die in infancy). His younger brother had been killed, absurdly, tragically, by a blow from a tennis ball. His best friend, Etienne de La Boétie, had died of the plague in his early thirties. And his father, whom he adored, had recently suffered a prolonged and agonizing death from a kidney stone. Moreover, violent religious warfare was spreading across the country, setting light to Montaigne's region, pitting Catholic against Protestant, father against son, massacre against murder.

And so in a Latin inscription he had made on the wall of his library after resigning from his job as a magistrate and retiring to his house, Montaigne had declared his intention to hide himself away, and crawl unburthened towards death:

> In the year of Christ 1571, aged thirty-eight, on the eve of the beginning of March, his birthday, Michel de Montaigne, worn out with the slavery of the court and of public service, and whilst still intact, retires to the bosom of the learned Muses, where in peace and security he hopes, if fate allows him, to pass what may be left of his life already more than half spent, consecrating this ancestral dwelling and sweet retreat to his liberty, tranquillity and repose.

The choice of his birthday expressed a melancholy fatalism: that this was the beginning of his cessation. And so Montaigne, soon to be pained with the illness that had killed his father, had retired to this round tower, to this third-floor room, to pass away, undisturbed, the little that 'may be left of his life'.

Montaigne is now renowned as the author of the *Essays*, perhaps, alongside the plays of Shakespeare and *Don Quixote*, one of the most important literary works of the Renaissance. In it he attempts to *essayer* or 'test' an amazing variety of topics, ranging from warfare to idleness, from drunkenness to thumbs. Begun a couple of years after Montaigne's retirement, yet continually added to over the twenty years up to his death, the *Essays* represent an amazing compendium of Renaissance beliefs and attitudes.

But Montaigne's erasing of the words of Lucretius from the ceiling of his library also marks an amazing reversal in Montaigne's outlook over the course of his writing – a shift from a philosophy of death to a philosophy of life.

Deeply influenced by the death of his father and the steadfastly stoical death of his friend La Boétie, Montaigne had initially retired with death uppermost on his mind: 'To Philosophize is to Learn to Die,' as he declares in the title of one of his first essays. But over the course of his writing, Montaigne turns his back on this pessimism and embraces a new philosophy, in which it is 'living happily, not . . . dying happily, that is the source of human happiness'. Like James Stewart's character in *It's A Wonderful Life*, Montaigne begins to reject despair and feel the texture of the simple fabric of existence. And, with this, his essays grow from simple distractions into a way of replaying, rewinding, and reliving his life as he lives it: 'I want to increase it in weight; I want to arrest the speed of its flight by the speed with which I seize it . . . The shorter my possession of life, the more deeply and fully I must make use of it.'

And Montaigne's writing overflows with life. In over a hundred essays and around half a million words he records every thought, every taste and sensation that crosses his mind. He writes essays on sleep and on sadness, on smells and friendship, on children and sex and death. And, as a final testament, he writes an essay on experience, in which he

5

contemplates the wonder of human existence itself.

And in the text of the *Essays* and his *Travel Journal* (recounting his trip to Italy), Montaigne explores the pains, paradoxes and pleasures of being. He asks whether you should jump or duck at the bang of an arquebus, or whether to stand still or run at the enemy. He tells how Plato says you shouldn't drink before you are eighteen, should drink moderately until forty, but after then get drunk as often as possible. He notes the beauty of the prostitutes of Florence ('nothing special') and the Italians' love of large breasts. He loses his wallet; he pokes himself in the eye. He goes sledging down Mont Cenis. He goes to Pisa and meets the learned Doctor Burro, who presents him with a book on the ebb and flow of the sea.

Yet amidst these infinite interests there remains a heart to Montaigne's enquiry: his own experience of himself. For Montaigne stands at the watershed of the two great intellectual movements of the past millennium: the darkened vaulting of medieval Christendom and the monstrous progeny of seventeenth-century science. In both of these, everyday life is, in a sense, relegated: in science into mechanism and matter; in religion into transitoriness and sin. Montaigne is like a man standing on a platform, waiting between these two trains. Yet during this silence, in the space of perhaps a few decades around the end of the sixteenth century, life begins to unfurl. For what Montaigne discovers is the power of the ordinary and the unremarkable, the value of the here-and-now. And central to this is the idea that each and every one of us – and he takes himself as the primary example – has a *particular* way of viewing the world. He says that he sees himself as 'a very ordinary person, except in this regard, *that I consider myself so*'.

Montaigne's writing could thus be said to be the first

sustained representation of human consciousness in Western literature. This is not to say that people had been unconscious in the periods before, or that accounts of individual lives had not been written, such as by Augustine or Abelard. But no one had paid such attention to the actual experience of living, or seen life as providing a moral lesson – in justifying political and religious tolerance and providing a reason to continue to live. The Christian Stoicism of the sixteenth century saw the body and the senses as something to overcome, something which we should become indifferent to, and life as something that could be easily relinquished, provided the moral and theological price was right. But Montaigne rejects this indifference and over the course of his essays finds the reason for living in the very experience of living itself. He ponders the odour of his doublet, the itching in his ear. He savours the wine and the water of the towns he visits ('smell of sulphur, a little saltiness'). He thinks that parasols burden the arm more than they relieve his head and notes the outcome of various enemas – 'farted endlessly'. He tickles himself. He dreams that he dreams. He even has himself awoken from sleep, 'so that I might gain a glimpse of it'.

For Montaigne, life is to be lived actively and not passively, a vitality that led even Nietzsche – not one to hand out compliments – to proclaim: 'That such a man wrote has truly augmented the joy of living on this earth . . . If I were set the task, I could endeavour to make myself at home in the world with him.'

❧

But there is another reason for listening to this sixteenth-century Gascon nobleman.

Modern philosophy – and some would say the modern world – starts some thirty years after Montaigne when Descartes sequesters himself in a small stove-heated room and asks himself what he considers to be the most fundamental philosophical question: what can we believe with *certainty*? The answer Descartes arrives at – thinking – in the form of the maxim *Cogito ergo sum* (I think, therefore I am), has been a hobby-horse for philosophers ever since. And the edifice that Descartes and other seventeenth-century philosophers build around it – the huge glass-and-steel cathedral of Reason – is one that has eclipsed Montaigne's more modest tower. As a result, he has silently slipped below our intellectual horizons: an eccentric provincial essayist, albeit one often confused with the Enlightenment political theorist Montesquieu.

But Montaigne can be seen to offer an alternative philosophy to that of Descartes, a more human-centred conception that lays no claim to absolute certainty, but that is also free from what some have seen as the implications of such claims: the totalitarian political movements of the twentieth century, and the individualist anomie of modern Western life.

For at the heart of Descartes' philosophy is the intellectual principle of division, an attempt to offer clarity in a world made uncertain by religious and political unrest. He thus states as part of his 'method' that intellectual problems should be 'divided' into 'as many parts as possible' and that we should accept as true only that which we can perceive 'very clearly and *distinctly*' – i.e. separate from other things. And this principle provides the foundation for his division of mind and body: he sees the mind as all 'one and the same', whereas he 'cannot think of any Corporeal or extended being which I cannot easily divide into Parts'. For Descartes, true knowledge thus amounts to a singular unambiguous vision: he uses the metaphor of a city designed by one 'single master', rather than evolving naturally and haphazardly through the work of 'different hands'.

Montaigne, by contrast, operates with an older, less cutting-edge, yet perhaps more venerable intellectual instinct: that of *proximity*. Rather than defining and dividing things, Montaigne wants to bring them together, get near to them, close to them, not least to himself. And rather than searching for certainties that divide him from the commonality, Montaigne see the principle of trust as of far greater importance; as he says at the start of his essays: 'You have here a book of *good faith*.' For Montaigne, human relations are the primal scene of knowledge: if trust is restored, agreement, tolerance, and hence truth will follow; the search for constancy and certainty strikes him as merely obstinacy in another guise. And here the differences in their characters and circumstances are revealing: Descartes on foreign soil, escaping into a small, isolated, stuffy room, stoically immune to 'passions' or 'cares' (a recent biography describes him as a 'a reclusive, cantankerous, and oversensitive loner'). Montaigne, by contrast, writing at the centre of the French Wars of Religion, and as a seigneur and a negotiator between the warring factions trying desperately to heal 'these divisions and subdivisions by which we are today torn apart'.

For in the midst of these wars Montaigne begins to see such conflict as fuelled by the search for political and religious certainty. And whereas some saw the unfeeling Stoicism of the ancients as an ideal, a moral philosophy that Descartes endorsed, Montaigne begins to see it as exacerbating the divisiveness of his time, cutting off men's awareness of themselves and their understanding of others, resulting in an acceptance and, indeed, an appetite for murder and gratuitous cruelty.

Montaigne therefore decides to look more locally for his morality, beginning by examining or *essaying* himself. And what he discovers is the imperceived experience of existence – imperceived because of centuries of Christian moralizing, but also because its ever-presentness has rendered it invisible. Whereas Descartes' division of mind and body separates him from other bodies and other people, Montaigne sees his own relationship to his body as opening a gateway to 'the universal pattern of the human', and as a consequence society at large. Self-knowledge thus leads us into ourselves, but then out of ourselves into others: we need to get to know ourselves before we can understand our fellow man – a logical paradox from a modern perspective, but not for Montaigne.

Montaigne's essays thus bring with them an acceptance of variation and difference, but a difference built around our similarities in the first place. He sees travel as a way 'to rub and polish our brains through contact with others' and writes in Italian when in Italy and in French when he returns to France. He collects Brazilian love songs from the New World, making him perhaps the first fan of world music. He admires the Turks' provision of hospitals for animals and wonders whether elephants have a religion. In short, Montaigne's scepticism arrives at sympathy rather than certainty, seeing our most obstinate beliefs as simply grounded in habit. And with this Montaigne's essays grow out of their stoical adolescence – their obsession with battlefields and military tactics – and instead begin to explore the mindset of friends and enemies, animals and cannibals, Catholics, Protestants and Jews – even asking himself: 'When I am playing with my cat, how do I know she is not playing with me?'

But, most of all, Montaigne develops a philosophy based on the things that lie around him: nourished by our natural capacities, uncontaminated by the artificial additives of Stoicism, dogmatism and doubt. Rather than seeking sanctuary in the cathedral of Reason, Montaigne combs the shoreline where death claws at life, and builds a shelter from what he finds there. It is formed of sand and seashells, of friendship and sex, of dancing, sleeping, watermelons and wine. It takes as its subjects a fall from his horse, the bang of an arquebus, his dog, his cat, his kidney stones and the sights and sounds that surround him. But it is also composed of himself and his book: a book, he says, that is 'consubstantial with its author, concerned only with myself, an integral part of my life', with which he paces out his days 'hand in hand'. Rather than reaching above ourselves in a search for certainty, Montaigne shows us where we already stand. And instead of seeking for truths beyond the human, he poses a simpler but far more important philosophical problem: 'Have I wasted my time?'

'We are never at home, we are always beyond ourselves.' Montaigne's writing is an attempt to return home, to come close to himself, to shadow himself as he climbs the stairs to his library and sits in his chair. But from there he reaches out to the reader in a gesture that is quintessentially social, introducing himself to ourselves, though not simply in terms of his thoughts but in terms of his house and his vineyards, his books and his writing, his handshake, his smile, and his chestnut-brown hair. We are, he says, 'marvellously corporeal', and our sense of life increases as we see this mirrored in the proximity of others – a truth he discovers within himself, but then expands to take in friends and family, servants and neighbours, Germans, Italians – even other creatures – and finally invokes in the intimacy between ourselves as readers and himself.

All the time reminding us that if you value a friend, you should meet with them; if you are fond of your children, eat with them; if there is someone you love, stand close to them, be near to them. And if you want to get back in touch with life – as Flaubert wrote to a depressed correspondent – 'read Montaigne . . . He will calm you . . . You will love him, you will see.'

I

Waking to the Sound of a Spinet

Springing from the flanks of the Puy de Sancy in the mountains of the Auvergne, the Dordogne curls intestinally through the broad belly of France. It swells at the tributes of the Cère and the Vézère before sliding westward towards Bordeaux and the large estuary of the Gironde, where in a final peristalsis it meets with the sea. It gives life to the region, brought boats for the wine, and in Roman times gave a literal meaning to this old land of waters: Aquitaine.

Montaigne was born between eleven o'clock and noon on 28 February 1533. It was a fairly eventful year. Henry VIII married Anne Boleyn and was excommunicated by the Pope for his insolence. A daughter, Elizabeth, would follow soon after. Atahualpa, the last Emperor of the Incas, was strangled by his Spanish captors, despite paying a ransom of a room full of gold. And in France, just as the Protestant theologian John Calvin was leaving, Catherine de' Medici arrived as the wife of Henry II, bringing with her a taste for artichokes and aspics, sweetbreads, truffles and custard, thus helping to put French cuisine on the map and giving her something to chew on as she pondered the next twist and turn in the battle between Protestants and Catholics as the century unravelled.

Montaigne was christened 'Michel Eyquem de Montaigne' – Eyquem being the surname that he was to drop, Montaigne the name of the noble château in which he was born. His family owed its fortune to the propitious location of Bordeaux as a port for the fruits of this fertile region. Between the twelfth and the fifteenth centuries Aquitaine (or Gascony or Guyenne as it was variously called) had been English, following the marriage of Eleanor of Aquitaine to Henry Plantagenet, the heir to the English throne. English rule had ended in 1453 when John Talbot was cut down at the battle of Castillon, a few miles south of Montaigne, thereby bringing an end to the Hundred Years War. But during this time Bordeaux had grown fat with the profits from the English taste for Gascony's light-coloured wine: *clairet*, or claret.

The English defeat had initially been disastrous for the economy, but trade gradually recovered. And after a lifetime trading wine, herring and blue woad-dye, and trading-up in terms of marrying a wealthy wife, in 1477 Montaigne's great-grandfather, the Bordeaux merchant Raymond Eyquem, bought the house and estate of Montaigne, its vines, mills and woods, for 900 francs. There is a marvellous story about Raymond on the day of completion entering the house with the vendor, the vendor leaving the house, and Raymond barricading the door and cracking open a bottle of wine. You can still visit the château. It stands a couple of miles north of the Dordogne on a windy plateau above a vine-covered hill (the name Montaigne means mount or mountain). The original house burnt down in 1885, and was replaced by a neo-Renaissance copy, but miraculously Montaigne's tower survived. (We can get a sense of how the house originally looked from early-nineteenth-century illustrations like the one at the beginning of this chapter.)

As owner of his noble house, Raymond and his descendants enjoyed the title of Seigneur or Lord of Montaigne. The role of seigneur essentially derived from feudal times in that as well as his own personal demense he owned the title to the lands around him. Annually he received a recognitive rent or *cens* from his tenants. And if a tenant sold a piece of land, the seigneur received a sum of up to 25 per cent of the price, or had the option of buying the land himself – and reorganizing and maximizing his leases was something that Montaigne's father, Pierre, was very effective in doing. And Montaigne, in turn, was to harvest the fruits of these investments in being the third generation to have his hands unsullied by trade, earning him the right to consider himself a true member of the nobility.

The seigneur exercised the right of 'common oven' over his tenants, requiring them to use his flour mills, and also his wine presses, and taking a cut as his due. And this economic power was reflected in his social standing in the local community. He was entitled to carry a sword and be first to receive communion. And at the château he would hear and pass judgement on the squabbles of his tenants – errant ploughs and wayward cows grazing where they shouldn't.

The seigneurie of Montaigne was carefully built up during the fifteenth and early sixteenth centuries, by Raymond and then his son, Grimon, and then his son Pierre, Montaigne's father. Pierre became the first in the family to take up the aristocratic occupation of bearing arms, the traditional role of the nobility, whose privileges, such as their tax-free status, descended from their military service to the King. Pierre fought in the wars between France and Italy in the early sixteenth century, and upon returning from Italy in 1528 at the age of thirty-three married Antoinette de Louppes (or Lopez) from another wealthy Bordeaux merchant family, possibly of Spanish Jewish descent. Two years later he, like his father, became first jurat and provost of Bordeaux, rising to become mayor in 1554, a position that Montaigne was also to occupy.

Montaigne clearly adored his father, describing him as 'the

best father that there ever was, and the most indulgent, even in his very old age'. He possessed the sort of eccentric vigour that most beloved fathers have, providing an admirable but not too intimidating act to follow. He made himself dumb-bells from canes filled with lead, and some shoes with leaded soles 'to make him lighter in running and jumping'. Even when he was past sixty he could vault over a table, climb stairs four steps at a time, and leap into the saddle in his furred gown. Montaigne tells how he was also, in his own way, interested in writing. He wrote a diary of his time in the Italian wars (something Montaigne was to imitate in his own journal of his trip to Italy), and he also kept a book in which every occurrence, no matter how trivial, was recorded; as Montaigne recalls: 'Our journeys our absences; marriages, deaths; the receiving of happy or unhappy news; the change of the principal servants – such matters. An ancient custom, that I think would be good to revive, each in his own house. And I think I am a fool to have neglected it.'

About his mother, Antoinette, Montaigne says little, and his relationship with her seems to have been rather cool. There is evidence of her unhappiness with the distribution of the family's wealth in her will. And it has been suggested that Montaigne found her less interesting than her swashbuckling husband, coming as she did from more mercantile stock. But she was alive when Montaigne wrote, which perhaps inhibited him, and in fact outlived him, living all the time in the château. One wonders whether Montaigne's tower gave him an escape from not only the naggings of politics and parliament, but also pressures closer to home.

Pierre and Antoinette had two sons who died in infancy before Michel was born, which may help to explain his father's indulgence towards him. But Michel became the eldest of eight siblings – Thomas (1534), Pierre (1535) Jeanne (1536), Arnaud (1541), Léonor (1552), Marie (1555) and Bertrand-Charles (1560) – a brood that made the early deaths of five of his six daughters perhaps even harder to bear. Of his sisters, Jeanne became a Protestant but had a daughter, Jeanne de Lestonnac, who founded the Company of Mary Our Lady and was later canonized by the Catholic Church. Léonor, who was almost twenty years younger than Montaigne, married a councillor at the Bordeaux parliament and had a daughter, also called Jeanne. Marie married in 1579 but died childless soon after.

Of his brothers, Thomas, who was only a year younger than Montaigne also became a Protestant, and it was at their sister Jeanne's house that Montaigne's friend La Boétie died, taking the time to upbraid Thomas for his Protestant opinions. Montaigne notes in an aside the fate of Thomas's estate in the Médoc, the long tongue of land that samples the Atlantic north of Bordeaux: 'By the seashore, my brother, the Seigneur d'Arsac, sees an estate he had there, buried under the sands which the sea spews before it; where the tops of some houses can no longer be seen; where his rents and domains are converted into pitiful barren pasturage.'

Pierre Jr was the seigneur of La Brousse near Montravel, a couple of miles to the south-east. Montaigne mentions him as a travelling companion during the civil wars, but he didn't marry and left few traces: an order for a suit of armour, his name in a book. It was his younger brother, Arnaud, who died when he was twenty-seven after being hit in the head by a tennis ball (heavier and more solid in those days). His death had an uncomfortable aftermath, however, in that a gold chain of Arnaud's was found amongst Montaigne's wife's possessions, leading some to suppose a relationship between the two. Others see it as a rather unseemly squabble over the deceased brother's property (the chain was eventually given to their mother, Antoinette, who claimed it as her own). Whether this incident was a symptom or the cause of Montaigne's slightly formal conduct towards his wife we shall never know. The youngest son, Bertrand-Charles, was seigneur of Mattecoulon, three miles to the north. He accompanied Montaigne on his travels to Italy and was clearly of a combative temperament, striking someone who insulted the Virgin Mary and killing a man in a duel.

But the Montaigne family's attentions were clearly lavished on their first-born son, Michel, or Michou as he was affectionately called. Montaigne's father seems to have been quite progressive by sixteenth-century standards. He didn't beat his son, and he thought children should not be woken violently from sleep 'in which they are plunged more deeply than we are'. Young Michel was thus gently roused by the music of an epinette, an early form of spinet, remarking, 'I was never without a man to do this for me.' Due to the popularity of humanistic ideas at the time, he was also brought up to speak only Latin. Whilst he was still 'at nurse', a tutor named Horstanus was appointed to instruct him in the language, and the servants were forbidden from speaking French within earshot. According to Montaigne, a Latin isogloss thus grew up around the château, 'where there still remain Latin names for artisans and tools that have taken root by usage'. He says he was six years old before he 'understood any more French or Perigordian than Arabic' and 'knew the location of the Capitol before that of the Louvre, and the Tiber before the

Seine'. And later in life, when his father, wracked by the pain of a kidney stone, fainted into his arms, he says it was a Latin swear word that escaped his lips.

But despite this pampering, Pierre insisted that his son should not consider himself separate from his Gascon inheritance. He was sent out to nurse as an infant and at his christening two local villagers held him over the font. This may look like a marvellous egalitarianism, but it was also intended as a reassuring symbol of Michel's eventual responsibilities when he took over as seigneur – often a time of great unease amongst the locals. Montaigne's early self thus seems to have been steeped in this exceptional upbringing, but also washed in the commonality of human experience, providing lessons that stayed with him for the rest of his life.

In 1539, at the age of six, Montaigne's humanistic education continued when he went to the Collège de Guyenne in Bordeaux, itself established in the year he was born and considered, according to Montaigne, to be the 'best in France'. Here the school day lasted from seven in the morning till nine at night, in an academic year that stretched for eleven months. At first, Latin instruction was through rote, with the teacher moving up through the benches in the classroom until the whole class were word-perfect. Then students moved on to reading and composition in both Latin and French. In the higher years they went on to study Cicero, Ovid and Lucan as well as history from Livy and Seneca. At the age of sixteen (or fourteen, depending on ability), philosophy was studied, mainly Aristotelian logic and physics and Greek mathematics. It was an elite education with a radically fashionable teacherly edge: Montaigne's schoolfriend Florimond de Raemond recalled how the staff refused to make the sign of a cross at the start of a lesson, describing it as 'mummery'.

During his time at the school Montaigne was fortunate enough to be taught by some of Europe's educational elite, such as the Scottish humanist George Buchanan, later tutor to Mary Queen of Scots and James I. Montaigne took part in plays written by Buchanan and was, it seems, a talented young actor. In 'advance of his age', he claims, he played the leading parts and was considered somewhat of a 'master-worker' of the dramatic arts. He observes, somewhat ruefully, that in antiquity the theatre was considered a perfectly respectable profession for an aristocratic young man to enter.

But to understand the broader aims of Montaigne's education, one needs to understand the importance of humanism as an intellectual force during the Renaissance. Originating in Italy in the late fourteenth century and sweeping across Europe in the two centuries after, humanism amounted to an attempt to imitate and revive the culture of antiquity which had been lost with the fall of the Roman Empire. It was this that provided the 'rebirth' central to the idea of Renaissance. At the heart of the movement was an emphasis on what was known as the *studia humanitatis* (grammar, rhetoric, literary studies and moral philosophy), as opposed to the *studia divinitatis* (theology and natural science) – very broadly, a shift from divinity and logic to language. Through their new linguistic prowess, humanists sought to recover the classical past, but also exploit these rhetorical and oratorical skills in contemporary political and diplomatic life.

At the intellectual heart of the movement was the belief that language – i.e. speech – was the defining characteristic of what it was to be human, the thing that separated us from animals. According to Cicero, 'Men most excel the beasts in this, that they can speak.' But the exciting implication of this was that by improving oneself linguistically – through translation, textual scholarship, and commenting upon ancient texts – one could improve oneself morally (in stark contrast to our spiritual state as inheritors of original sin). Man could therefore develop, move further away from animals, and even approach perfection through the pursuit of eloquence – the central goal of humanist study, what the German humanist Johannes Santritter called 'the queen of all things'.

Montaigne's education thus reflects this ideal of an attainable perfection through eloquence. In class he would have been expected to learn rhetorical figures and tropes, and examine letter-writing manuals – for instance, *On Copiousness* by the Dutch humanist Erasmus, which gave 195 examples of the ways in which one might express pleasure at receiving a letter: 'Your letter has delighted me greatly', 'Your paper has imbued me with ineffable delight', 'What clover is to bees, what willow boughs are to goats, what honey is to the bear, your letter is to me' . . . and so on.

Pupils would then be expected to hone and rewrite their own compositions – a process that we can see at work in Montaigne's life's work: the steadily accumulating versions of the *Essays*. And through these exercises pupils were also drawn into the moral and political orbit of antiquity: rehearsing in their own strict classes the classical and Stoic lessons that made one into a man.

'Yet for all that,' Montaigne reflects, 'it was still a school.' And he remains mindful of the downside to this heady cultural optimism, in terms of the unrealistic expectations that it raised. Despite his precocity in Latin, Montaigne felt he gained little from his studies: he says his father reaped 'no fruit' from his investment because of his own 'sterile and unsuitable soil'. And during his schooldays, Montaigne felt himself toiling under an uncomfortable yoke of learning. He clearly found school rather boring, leaving at the age of thirteen. And in an essay 'Of the Education of Children' he berates the teaching establishment for their sadistic tendencies – 'intoxicated with their own rage' – and criticizes the 'torture' and 'hard labour' that constitutes the essential part of education's necessary demolition of the will.

Asking himself what he was fit for when he was younger, Montaigne answers: 'For nothing.' He describes himself as the dullest and slowest not only of his brothers but of all the boys in his region. And despite his admiration for his father, he reveals that 'he who left me in charge of my house predicted that I would ruin it'. Proof of this is given in the will that his father made in 1561, naming his wife as the inheritor of his estate; only later, in 1567, did he change it to name his eldest son. And Montaigne's apparent lack of promise is shown in the fact that our knowledge of him dissipates in the years immediately after his schooling, where he spent his time possibly studying law in Paris or Toulouse. He was saved when an uncle stooped to his aid, securing for him a post in the newly created Court at Périgueux in 1554, which a few years later would merge with the parliament at Bordeaux.

2

Because It Was Him; Because It Was Me

Perhaps the most famous of all Montaigne's essays is that 'Of Friendship', dealing with his relationship with Etienne de La Boétie. For five years he says he enjoyed the 'sweet companionship' of his friend; the days following his death being 'nothing more than smoke, nothing more than a dark and dreary night'.

Montaigne worked at the Bordeaux parliament for thirteen tedious years, dealing with mainly complex civil legal cases in the Chambre des Enquêtes (chamber of petitions) rather than the more important cases in the Grand' Chambre. But his boredom was alleviated by the friendship he struck up with La Boétie, a fellow counselor and a precocious humanist and author of a treatise against tyranny. Their friendship lasted from 1558 until La Boétie's death in 1563; yet Montaigne's grief for his friend never ends. His most famous sentence describing the essence of their affection was composed over the two decades between the time he first started writing the essays around 1572 and his final additions to the text up to twenty years later. At first he writes, 'If pressed to say why I loved him, I feel that it cannot be expressed.' But then he adds the phrase: 'except by saying: because it was him; because it was me', with each part of the addition being written in a different pen. And this agrees with the pattern of increasing openness and emotional honesty we see in Montaigne's writing as it matures over time. In 1580 he describes the fact that most of his children had died in infancy: 'but one single daughter who has escaped that misfortune, is more than six years old, and has never been guided or chastised for her childish faults'. But returning to the line again in the years before he dies, Montaigne encircles her name within the arms of his sentence: 'but *Léonor*, one single daughter . . .'

La Boétie influenced the *Essays* in a number of important ways. He left Montaigne his books and papers, which served as the foundation of his library. He provided a Stoic model to which Montaigne initially attempted to adhere. And his death created an absence that Montaigne attempted to fill with writing. He says that he would have preferred to have written letters rather than essays, yet lacked an addressee: 'a certain relationship to lead me on, to sustain me, and raise me up. For I cannot talk to the wind.' Relaxing in a spa in Italy some eighteen years after La Boétie's death, Montaigne was suddenly overcome with grief for his dead friend: 'and felt like that for so long, without recovering, that it caused me much pain'.

❧

Etienne de La Boétie was born in 1530 at Sarlat, thirty miles east of Montaigne on the Dordogne. His family was well connected: his father was assistant to the Governor of Périgord and his mother the sister of the president of the Bordeaux parliament. Orphaned at an early age, he was educated by his uncle, a priest, before entering the university of Orléans to study law. There, he was taught by the future Protestant martyr Du Bourg and it was probably during this period that he wrote his famous discourse against tyranny, *On Voluntary Servitude*. It was a treatise probably inspired by the ferment surrounding the suppression of the salt tax riots in Bordeaux in 1548, but it also looks forward to Enlightenment ideas of natural liberty, fraternity and freedom from subjection. Men are dulled, says La Boétie, by custom and ideology into an acceptance of tyrannical rule. Yet through solidarity and passive resistance they can achieve its overthrow. In this sense *On Voluntary Servitude* stood as an antidote to Machiavelli's *The Prince* (1513), which had argued for the necessity of autocratic rule to maintain power. La Boétie, more idealistically, senses the incipient power and rights of the people: Montaigne says La Boétie would rather have been born at Venice (a republic) than at Sarlat. But although the text of *On Voluntary Servitude* was widely circulated – Montaigne says that he had read it before they met – it was only published posthumously, in 1574.

After graduation La Boétie became a counselor at the Bordeaux parliament, where his talents were soon recognized. He was entrusted with a mission to Henry II to petition for regular payments to the court, and he became a respected political negotiator: at Agen to the south-west of Bordeaux he arranged that Protestants should be allowed access to churches when they weren't being otherwise used. And during this time he also made his mark as a humanist, translating Xenophon and Plutarch from Greek into French.

In 1557 Montaigne joined the Bordeaux parliament and soon became aware of his future friend, as La Boétie soon became aware of him, and when they finally encountered each other, Montaigne recorded:

> We sought each another before we met, from reports we had each heard of the other . . . And at our first meeting, which happened by chance at a great feast and town gathering, we found ourselves so taken with each other, so well acquainted, so bound together, that from that moment on nothing could be as close as we were to one another . . .

They soon became inseparable: a pair of wealthy, well-connected men about town, La Boétie even dedicating three Latin poems to his younger, more hedonistic friend, praising his 'fiery energy', but upbraiding him for his sensual desire.

But in August 1563 La Boétie died. We know the details of his death from a letter that Montaigne wrote to his father, telling of his final days and published at the end of his posthumous edition of his friend's works in 1572.

On Monday 9 August La Boétie was taken ill with stomach pains, having recently returned from a mission to Agen to the south-east of Bordeaux, where plague as well as religious unrest was rife. Montaigne tells how he had invited him to dinner, but on hearing his friend was unwell went to see him and found him 'much changed' – suffering from dysentery and stomach cramps, yet blaming himself for exercising the day before whilst wearing only a doublet and silk shirt. Montaigne encouraged him to get away from Bordeaux all the same, for the houses round about were also visited by the plague, and to go to Germignan, six miles away, to stay with his sister, Jeanne de Lestonnac. Besides, he added, a journey on horseback can sometimes help with such complaints.

The next day, however, Montaigne received word from La Boétie's wife that he had deteriorated during the night. She called a physician and an apothecary but urged Montaigne to come. La Boétie was overjoyed to see his friend and persuaded Montaigne to stay. Montaigne left the following day but went to see him again on Thursday, and again found his condition worrying. He was rapidly losing blood and was very weak. Montaigne went away but returned again on Saturday and after that never left his side.

On Sunday La Boétie lost consciousness for a while and when

he came to said that he had seemed to be in a 'thick cloud and dense fog' but felt no pain. He continued to sicken, and called for his wife and uncle to be brought into the room, so that they might hear what he had set down in his will. Montaigne said that this would alarm them – and then La Boétie broached the subject that was quickly becoming unignorable:

And then he asked whether we hadn't been somewhat alarmed by his fainting. 'It is nothing, my brother,' I told him: 'these accidents happen with such illnesses.' 'True, my brother,' he said, 'it would be nothing, even if it should happen to be the thing you most fear.' 'For you,' I replied, 'it might be a good thing, but the loss would be mine, being thereby deprived of so great, so wise, and so resolute a friend, the like of which I would never be able to find again.'

La Boétie then thanked his uncle for bringing him up and told his wife that he had willed her 'such portion of my estate as I give to you, and be contented with it, though it is very inadequate to your merits'.

He then turned to Montaigne:

'My brother,' he said, 'for whom I have so entire a love, and whom I chose from so many men, thinking to renew with you that virtuous and sincere friendship which, due to the vices of the age, has grown to be almost unknown to us, and which now only exists in certain traces in our memory of antiquity, I beg you, as a sign of my affection, to accept my library . . . a slender offering, but offered in good will, and appropriate to you, given the affection you have for letters. It will be a memorial of your old companion.'

Montaigne responded by praising La Boétie for his 'admirable fortitude', and for providing a philosophical model that he vowed to emulate 'when my turn came', all of which, he insisted was, 'the real object of our studies and of philosophy'. La Boétie then took Montaigne by the hand, saying that his death would in a sense be a deliverance from the vexations of life, confident in the fact that he would meet God in the 'abode of the blessed'. Montaigne described him as 'a soul full of repose, tranquillity and assurance', 'steadfast' and full of 'eloquence' to the end.

Eventually, however, the illness overwhelmed him to the extent that they had to force his mouth open to make him drink, La Boétie asking pitifully but stoically: '*An vivere tanti est?*' (Is life worth so much?). Finally, he called for Montaigne, saying: 'My brother . . . stay close to me, please.' But at this point a discordant note enters Montaigne's account – perhaps the real feelings and terrified panic of a dying man? La Boétie becomes deranged, appealing to Montaigne: 'My brother, my brother, do you refuse me a place?'

But then, finally:

> he began to rest a little, which revived us in our hopes, so much so that I left the room and rejoiced at this with Madame de La Boétie. But an hour or so later, he spoke my name once or twice, and then, heaving a long sigh to himself, he gave up his soul, at three o'clock on the Wednesday morning, the 18th of August 1563, after having lived thirty-two years, nine months, and seventeen days.

Montaigne's letter is clearly a moving testament to his friend. But the question that inevitably raises itself is to what extent was there more than friendship at stake – that is to say, was it a platonic relationship or a romantic one?

The idea that the two men's relationship was a homosexual one is by no means implausible, but neither is it necessarily the case: Montaigne later adds to his essay a reference to: 'that other Greek licence . . . justly abhorred by our conscience', meaning homosexuality, a crime one of his schoolmasters, Marc-Antoine Muret, was accused of, for which he was forced to flee France. And Montaigne talks about friendship as holding everything in common: 'wills, thought, opinions, possessions, wives, children, honour, and life'. So his conception of friendship was not necessarily inimical to marriage, and La Boétie was married at the time that they were friends (although, of course, this in itself doesn't rule out a relationship between them, even an unconsummated one).

But what we as modern readers perhaps fail to recognize in the intensity of Montaigne's friendship with La Boétie is the influence of classical ideas of friendship, which descended from Aristotle and Cicero and which saw friendship as a relationship of distinct significance – in the words of Aristotle, the existence of 'one soul in two bodies'. In the classical sense, friendship was special because it was free from the vested interests of family and marriage: i.e. one gained nothing tangible from it, such as inherited wealth or children. And this idea often combined with a Stoic impulse in the sense that true friendship was most clearly manifested *after* death, when one's affections stood no chance of being reciprocated. Jean-Jacques Boissard's *Emblèmes Latins* (1588) thus includes an emblem entitled 'Perfect is the friendship that lives after death', which shows two friends sitting either side of a vine-covered tree. One of them is dressed as a Roman solder, the other wearing the gown of a dying man. The accompanying text explains:

> The friend his naked, poor and fragile friend embraces:
> And grows affection where affliction grows:
> Small is the virtue that assists the living,
> Of a weak friendship, but that which stays
> The same after death, achieves perfection.

But perhaps the most famous representation of this humanistic idea of friendship is provided by Hans Holbein's *The Ambassadors*, which was painted in April 1533, a few months after Montaigne was born. Jean de Dinteville was the French ambassador to the English court and his friend Georges de Selve was Bishop of Lavaur and also a humanist scholar, having translated Plutarch's series of dual biographies, *Parallel Lives*. The portrait was painted during a visit Selve paid to Dinteville in London, just before he left to take up the position of ambassador to Venice. So the painting, probably commissioned by Selve, was a record, despite their impending separation, of their friendship, one document describing Selve as Dinteville's '*intime ami*'.

But scholars have been intrigued by the symbols of division in the painting. On the lower shelf there is a lute with a broken string (a traditional symbol of discord), some flutes (associated with war), a terrestrial globe centred on Rome and opposite it a copy of a Lutheran hymnal; dividers; and a mathematics textbook, Peter Apian's *A New and Thorough Instruction in all Mercantile Calculations* of 1527, itself opened to an entry on division.

What the painting therefore seems to be saying is that humanist friendship has the power to rise above social and political conflict – and here we are reminded of the tense negotiations around Henry VIII's divorce, negotiations of which Dinteville, as ambassador, would have been well aware. And it is perhaps no accident that art historians have interpreted the two figures in an almost marital pose: male, humanistic friendship being seen to transcend the trouble and strife of matrimony.

But this message is further complicated by the astronomical clocks on top of the table. When looked at in detail it emerges that they all show contradictory times: the pillar dial showing a time of 9 a.m. on 10 April, or 3 p.m. on 15 August; the polyhedral dial and the celestial globe showing times of 10.30 a.m. and 2.40 p.m., respectively. What this suggests is that despite our instinctive desire to see the painting as a record of a specific time and location, as if it were a photograph, it has in fact an altogether more ambitious meaning. What we begin to realize is that that Jean de Dinteville and Georges de Selve are peering at us from *outside time*.

Dinteville and Selve are thus pictured in the true colours of the afterlife, their friendship rising above political and religious division, but also beyond death itself. And it is this that helps to explain the strange anamorphic skull that spills across the bottom of the picture. Traditionally, a skull would have been included in a picture to represent the transience of human existence; but here this message is reversed: it is the friendship of Dinteville and Selve that is more real, more long-lasting than death, with the result that death itself becomes ephemeral – as if passing at speed across the plane of the painting. The mortal world thus exists in another dimension, almost as if it were from a different painting that had been leaned up against this one (something a busy painter like Holbein must have seen often). And if we look more closely at the painting we soon become aware of its more general lack of moorings: the floor recedes into the darkness of space; the curtain reveals only a crucifix at the top left-hand side. The only sure coordinate is the friendship between Dinteville and Selve, which knits them together across the vast interstices of eternity. As they look down upon us from their immortal perspective, they can no longer discern the skull at the bottom of the picture: they can no longer see Death (and of course the dark irony of the painting is that as we slowly decline our heads towards the floor, the rest of us can).

Montaigne's letter describing La Boétie's death thus represents a dual portrait similar to Holbein's, intended to capture Montaigne and La Boétie's shared sense of Christian and Stoic resolve: of friendship perfected by death. And after La Boétie's death, Montaigne fulfils one of the traditional roles of friendship – to selflessly, stoically, complete your friend's work, seeing through the press La Boétie's *Oeuvres*, the final fruits of his humanistic prowess.

But the question that remains is whether such humanistic memorializing can ever really make up for the physical loss of a friend: something that Holbein's portrait anticipates but does not face; and perhaps it's the thing that breaks through La Boétie's Stoic resolve in his final desperate plea to be afforded 'a place'? Montaigne's continued, anguished return to the memory of his friend suggests an unease with this humanistic credo. And in his essay 'Of Friendship', begun a few years after his letter was first published, and nearly ten

years after La Boétie death, Montaigne refers to the 'faint and forceless' discourses 'that stern antiquity have left concerning this subject'. Here, instead of simply memorializing La Boétie in words, Montaigne announces his intention to reprint his *On Voluntary Servitude* next to his own essays at the centre of his first book, switching from literary precedents and instead comparing himself to a painter:

Considering the way in which a painter I had employed planned his work, I had a desire to imitate him. He chooses the best spot, in the middle of each wall, to situate a picture that is elaborated with all his ability; and the space around it he fills with grotesques – that is to say, fantastic paintings whose charm lies in their variety and strangeness.

And what are these essays, in truth, but grotesque and monstrous bodies, pieced together out of divers members, without a definite shape, without any order, logic, or proportion, except a fortuitous one? . . . In the second aspect I go with my painter, but I fall short in the other and better part: for my ability is not such that I could dare attempt a picture that is rich, finished, and formed in accordance with art. It has occurred to me to borrow one from Etienne de La Boétie, which will honour the rest of this work.

The discourse of La Boétie's Christian humanism in a sense celebrated absence – the 'purity' of friendship arising from its lack of familial, matrimonial, and physical ties. But here it is exactly the physical convergence of the two texts that seems to interest Montaigne – less a sense of two souls in one body than of two bodies meeting in one book. Here La Boétie's classical presence casts a lustre over Montaigne, and Montaigne turns to his friend, introducing him as if he were there in person: 'Listen now to this boy of eighteen . . .'

But at the last minute the divisive politics of the sixteenth century forced themselves between them. In 1578, just when Montaigne was about to go to press, the Huguenot minister Simon Goulart included *On Voluntary Servitude* in his *Memoirs of the State of France under Charles IX*, a collection of anti-royalist tracts, and by placing it alongside them – 'mixing it up with their own scribblings' as Montaigne says – effectively claimed La Boétie as one of their own. On 7 May 1579 the Bordeaux parliament ordered the *Memoirs* to be burned.

Montaigne seemed to have no option other than to distance himself from his friend's text, denying it a place and replacing it with a selection of La Boétie's sonnets. But to mark its absence, in the place where La Boétie's words should have run on from his own, Montaigne inserts a divider: three cold and distant five-fingered stars marking the cold and irredeemable distance of his loss.

Like hands reaching out but never touching they symbolize the final pessimism of 'Of Friendship', which ends light years away from the optimistic humanism of Holbein, Dinteville and Selve. Montaigne initially attempts to hold on to this sense of Christian Stoicism, but finds it slipping through his fingers: it is as if Holbein's painting has been twisted and sheared to reveal the skull at its heart. And by 1580 and the subsequent editions of the *Essays*, Holbein's optimistic ontology seems to be overturned: death and division are again in the ascendant. La Boétie is not only a lost friend, but also a lost world – he was 'one of the old stamp'. And looking back to his upbringing among the ancients – Lucullus, Metellus and Scipio – Montaigne concludes that ultimately, despite their historical fame, like his friend Etienne,

> They are dead. So, indeed, is my father, as absolutely dead as they are, and as distant from me and from life in eighteen years as they are in sixteen hundred.

And as if to confirm the inhospitable chill of the universe, Montaigne later tells how the mathematician Jacques Peletier, the author of a treatise 'On the Meeting of Lines' (1579), described to him the cosmic loneliness of an asymptotic curve, reaching out to a line that it will never meet:

> I have been told that in Geometry (which thinks it has reached the high point of certainty among the sciences) can be found irrefutable demonstrations that subvert the truth of experience: as Jacques Peletier told me in my house, that he had found two lines which travel towards each other as if to meet, but which he proved would never be able to touch, not even unto eternity . . .

Returning to 'Of Friendship', in the face of the widening distance of his loss, it would seem Montaigne can do little other than fall back on the slender reconciliations of his pen: 'Because it was him; because it was me.'

3

To Jump or Duck at the Bang of an Arquebus

In the years following La Boétie's death Montaigne's life flowed through the banks and channels of its natural inclination. In September 1565 he married Françoise de La Chassaigne, the daughter of an important Bordeaux family; her father was a counselor of the Bordeaux parliament and later its president. Montaigne worked tirelessly as a counselor himself, although failing to achieve promotion to the upper court. And he embarked on a scholarly project, translating, at his father's request, the *Natural Theology, or Book of Creatures* of the medieval theologian Raymond Sebond.

But on 18 June 1568, on the same day that Montaigne in Paris dedicated his translation of Sebond to him, his father died. On hearing the news Montaigne returned to the château and with his brothers oversaw the execution of his father's will. And in April 1570 Montaigne resigned his post in the Bordeaux parliament in order to take up his inheritance – the title of Seigneur de Montaigne. His homecoming was marked tragically, however, with the death that summer of his first-born daughter, Thoinette.

Perhaps by way of distraction, Montaigne turned his attention to the tower at the south-eastern corner of the château – previously 'the most useless place in the house' – turning it into a library – 'a handsome one among country libraries' – carrying La Boétie's books up the stairs and arranging them on his shelves:

> It is on the third floor of a tower. On the first [ground] is my chapel, on the second a bedroom with a dressing-room, where I often retire, to be alone. Above it is a large

drawing-room . . . There I pass most of the days of my life and most of the hours of the day. I am never there at night. Adjoining the library is a neat little study with a fireplace for the winter, very pleasantly lit . . . My library is round in shape, the only flat side being that needed for my table and my chair; and in its roundness offering me a view of my books, arranged on five shelves all around. It has three views of rich and easy prospect, and sixteen paces in diameter. In winter I am not there so often, for my house is perched on a hill, as its name implies, and no part is more exposed than this, which I like, for being rather difficult to get to and a little out of the way, both for the benefit of the exercise, and because I can take a step back from business.

Here he often slept, listening to the bell that rang out the Angelus every morning and every evening, with such a resounding peal that at first he thought he would not be able to put up with it, only to find that after a while 'I hear it without offence, and often without waking'.

But in retiring to his house, and surrounding himself with the texts of the ancients, Montaigne was also rehearsing a classical ideal, that of the Roman statesman exchanging the busy life of the Senate for his country villa, replacing *negotium* (public affairs) with *otium* (leisure). However, Montaigne was not sustained by reading alone. And in his essay 'Of Idleness' – probably the first that he wrote – he gives voice to the frustration that such inactivity can bring:

Lately when I retired to my house, determined, as far as I could, to worry about nothing except spending the little that remained of my life in isolation and repose, I thought that I could not more benefit my mind than to allow it to entertain itself at its leisure, and thus to come to rest and settle within itself, which I hoped it might do more easily, becoming heavier and riper with time. But instead I find – *Variam semper dant otia mentem* [Leisure always breeds wandering thoughts (Lucan)] – that, rather, like a runaway horse, it gives itself a hundred more troubles . . . and creates so many chimeras and fantastic monsters, one on top of the other, without order or design; and so in order to reflect on their stupidity and strangeness at leisure, I have begun to put them in writing, hoping in time to make my mind ashamed of itself.

Clearly, a life of pure *otium* did not suit the rather fidgety Montaigne, whose legs and feet, he says, dance and jig 'like quicksilver'. Nor did he relish the vexations of managing his estate. He had already tried his hand as an editor and translator and so writing seemed to present itself as a suitably noble occupation. His tower gave him a certain freedom from the pressures of domesticity, and his reading provided him with examples of the sort of thing he might do – the collections of quotations and exempla from the classics that spread humanistic culture, such as the *Colloquies* and *Adages* of Erasmus, but more recently the translation by Jacques Amyot of the *Moralia* of Plutarch in 1572 – similarly discursive disquisitions on a wide variety of themes.

But as the new head of his noble house, Montaigne had also become a member of the *noblesse d épée* (nobility of the sword), whose privilege and sense of honour was derived from war – as he says: 'the proper, the only, the essential, form of nobility in France'. But warring was an expensive profession, one not necessarily open to Montaigne's more average means. (In fact, his active military service – he was in attendance at the sieges of La Fère and Rouen, though in what capacity is unclear – seems to have been undistinguished.) Writing therefore presented itself as an alternative form of advancement to that of the military. But Montaigne could not that easily relinquish his hold on the traditions of nobility and, with them, the memory of his father. And so as he sat down and began 'meddling with writing', Montaigne attempted to give both arms and letters their due by turning his attention to war.

Montaigne's earliest essays are characterized by their obsession with battle plans and tactics, arquebuses, lances and the generalissimos of old. He composes an essay comparing 'ancient arms with ours' which is unfortunately stolen by a servant. But one can sense where Montaigne's sympathies lie when he describes the awesome power of the Romans' flaming spear or *phalarica*, or their skill with the javelin in pinning armed men together like a kebab. In contrast he sees the pistol, despite its loud bangs, as a 'weapon of very little effect, and hope that some day we shall do away with it'.

In his treatment of warfare, Montaigne stays close to one of the principles of humanistic study: the idea that the past has lessons for the present, or as Cicero famously put it: 'History, the teacher of life'. The longest sentence in the *Essays*, conquering more than a page and a half, is thus in praise of Alexander, 'the greatest and most experienced captain in the world'. And Montaigne goes on to inspect the ancients' equipment admiringly. He describes the woven Parthian armour which looked like feathers, and how some nations had helmets made from cork. He tells how Caesar's armour was multicoloured and how the Great Alexander went without it from time to time. By contrast the ancient Gauls' armour was so heavy that they were unable to hurt or be hurt, but once toppled couldn't get up again. And turning to the present day, Montaigne condemns the fashion among the nobility for leaving everything till the very last minute:

> It is a lamentable and effeminate custom of the nobility of our time to not put on their armour until the moment of most extreme necessity, and to take it off again, as soon as there is any sign of the danger being over. From which arise many disorders. For, with everyone shouting and running for his arms when they should be charging, some are still lacing their cuirass when their companions are already routed . . . Our troops are nowadays so confused and encumbered with the clutter of baggage and servants, who cannot themselves be separated from their masters, because they carry their arms.

Montaigne broods on the logical conclusion to all this commotion – where a horse might end up carrying thirty-five stone of knight, arms and armour – and predicts the invention of the tank: 'Now that our arquebusiers are so much in credit, I think that someone will find some invention to imprison us for our safety, and will drag us to the war in castles, like those with which the ancients loaded their elephants.'

In these first essays Montaigne thus strikes a Stoic note, in line with the martial creed to which he felt he belonged. In this, warfare was seen as an essentially noble pursuit, where Stoic constancy was manifested through the doughty withstanding of pain. He thus recalls the bravado of the ancient Florentines who rang a bell called the Martinella to inform their enemies of their warlike intents, and the chivalric sang-froid of Captain Bayard – The Knight without Fear and Reproach – who asked to be propped up against a tree and left to die facing his foe. And Montaigne denounces all forms of martial trickery, such as that of Cleomenes, who slaughtered his enemy in darkness during a ceasefire, saying that the seven-day truce he had agreed to had failed to mention the nights.

But what soon emerges from Montaigne's writing is a tension between this *code d'honneur* and the reality of sixteenth-century battle. For what Montaigne discerns is the demise of a noble martial culture in the face of what has been called a 'revolution' in warfare over the sixteenth century. During this time armies greatly expanded: the standing French army grew from 50,000 in the mid-sixteenth century, to 80,000 after the Wars of Religion, to more than 100,000 by the 1630s. And with it warfare became a more bureaucratic and logistical exercise, with a greater emphasis on sieges and fortifications. But a key element in this growth was the introduction of firearms, and most notably the arquebus, the AK47 of its time.

The arquebus came into use towards the end of the fifteenth century. It was a smooth-bore weapon about three feet long, fired by pulling on an S-shaped pivot that lowered a piece of smouldering hemp into a firing pan. It was much more quickly mastered than a longbow, requiring less physical strength, and it was quicker to reload than a crossbow, which left you desperately rewinding after you had shot your bolt. It was notoriously inaccurate over a distance greater than fifty yards – Don John of Austria grimly advised that 'you should never fire your arquebus until you are near enough to be splashed with the blood of your enemy' – and it tended to be unreliable, often leaving you with only a flash in the pan. But over a limited range it was lethal, the soft one-ounce lead balls easily penetrating armour and flesh. The stage was therefore set for a huge escalation in the scale and intensity of conflict. Armies could be raised quickly, with all and sundry enrolled in the arquebusiers' ranks. At the battle of Pavia in 1525, the decisive engagement in the Italian wars in which Montaigne's father fought, 1,500 arquebuses let rip against the French with devastating effect. And with this, according to one observer, 'the practice of valorous courage . . . utterly perished', the field 'covered with the pitiful slaughter of noble horsemen and piles of dying horses'.

This proliferation of firearms initially received much negative comment. In his *Art of War* (1521), Machiavelli remarked that arquebuses were only fit for scaring peasants, and in a hypothetical set-piece gave them a minor role. Others noted their effectiveness but lamented the debasement of the military vocation. To the nobility, the outcome of a battle should reflect the valour of the combatants, as manifested in their skill in horsemanship and the handling of arms. The arrival of massed ranks of unskilled arquebusiers, any of whom might take out a general with a lucky hole in one, brought a degrading arbitrariness into the equation, as Don Quixote lamented in his own discourse on weapons:

Happy were the ages past, whilst strangers to those infernal instruments of artillery . . . for, often in the heat of that courage and resolution that fires and animates the gallant breast, there comes a random ball, how or from whence no man can tell, shot off, perhaps by one that fled and was afraid at the flash of his own accursed machine, and in an instant, puts an end to the future of a man who deserved to live for ages.

Captain Bayard was said to have dispatched any arquebusier that fell into his hands, only to have his own spine shattered by an arquebus ball in return. And in his memoirs, Montaigne's fellow Gascon Marshal Monluc bitterly laments the arrival of this 'cursed instrument' without which 'many brave men wouldn't be dead at the hands of those weaker and more cowardly than themselves'. He recalls how during the siege of Rabastens, 'an arquebus-shot clapt into my face', caving in his features and reducing his cheek-bones to splinters. Rabastens was nevertheless taken, and made to pay:

> My Lieutenant . . . came to see if I was dead, and said to me: 'Sir, cheer up your spirits and rejoice, we have entered the castle, and the soldiers are laying about them, putting all to the sword; and assure yourself we will avenge your injury.' I then said to him, 'Praised be God that I see the Victory is ours before I die. I now care not for death. I beseech you return back, and as you have ever been my friend, so now do me that act of friendship as not to offer so much as one man to escape with his life.'

Not knowing who had pulled the dastardly trigger, Monluc thus had them all slaughtered. The traditional proportionality of war as a contact sport – an eye for an eye, a tooth for a tooth – seemed to be at an end.

An illustration to Hans von Gersdorff's *Fieldbook of Wound Surgery* of 1528 helps to communicate this sense of the arbitrary, impersonal horrors of sixteenth-century warfare. Gersdorff's injured, although still-standing, man shows the type of traumas received on the battlefield. He takes up a classical anatomical pose but has a distinctly war-torn look. But what is interesting is the distribution of his injuries.

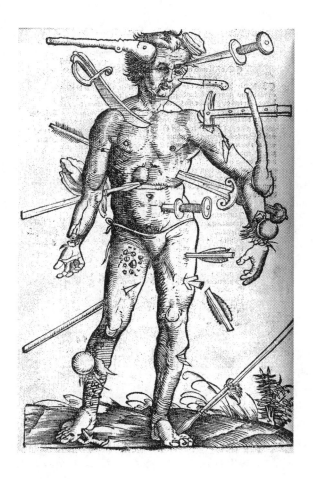

Hand-held weapons have hit their mark, the sword piercing his torso and the club and daggers stabbing and battering him about the head. Arrows have a varied effect, one hitting him square in the chest, one piercing his thigh. But in terms of firearms their distribution is far less accurate. His thigh is peppered with shot, a nasty though not necessarily fatal wound; and two artillery balls have hit his extremities, albeit with devastating effect, but some distance away from his vital organs. The moral seems to be that firepower brings with it a terrible destructive force, yet one that is far more open to chance. It all depends on where you happened to be standing at the time.

❧

It is this randomly cruel, impersonal world that Montaigne confronts in his *Essays*. For Montaigne, the introduction of firearms represents an exponential increase in the unpredictability of warfare – less a proving ground for the nobility, more a game of Russian roulette. He looks back wistfully to the ancient Galatians who forsook 'treacherous flying weapons', and admires Alexander's refusal to throw his lance at the fleeing Orodes, preferring to meet his enemy 'man to man'.

And he brings the issue to a head by asking whether it is best to jump or duck to avoid the shot of an arquebus, or simply stand still. He relates how, during the invasion of Provence by Charles V in 1536, the Marquis de Guast was spotted emerging from behind a windmill. A cowardly gunner took aim with a culverin, yet the Marquis saw the match applied and jumped aside, the shot piercing the air in the place he had just stood. Yet during the 1517 siege of Mondolfo, Lorenzo de Medici saw the lighting of a gun aimed at him and instead opted to duck – this time the shot only grazing the top of his head. Yet Montaigne remarks that, given the inaccuracy of sixteenth-century firearms, especially over a distance, such evasive measures might just as easily place one into the bullet's path: 'Fortune favoured their fright but on another occasion the same movement would be just as likely to throw them into danger as save them from it.'

But for Montaigne this unpredictability also has a number of implications. Firstly, it undermines ideas of Protestant predestination – everything is far more open to chance, a randomness that he emphasizes in the essay that he places at the start of his work: 'By Diverse Means We Arrive at the Same End'. But, secondly, it provides a moral lesson. In *The Prince* (1513), the sixteenth century's most famous manual of Realpolitik, Niccolò Machiavelli had argued that a ruler could manipulate fortune through the exercise of *virtù*, a ruthless decisiveness in which Christian morality played no part. But for Montaigne modern armaments make a mockery of such endeavours, especially when the exercising of *virtù* – attempting to leap out of the way – might just as easily land you in the line of fire. Equally for those firing the guns, taking aim amounts to little more than a shot in the dark:

> It is clearly apparent that we may more assure ourselves
> of the sword we hold in our hand, than of a bullet that
> escapes from a pistol, in which there are many factors –
> the powder, the stone, and the wheel – which if the least
> of them were to fail, your fortune would fail also.

The fickleness of gunpowder thus undermines even the best-laid battle-plans. Montaigne records how during the siege of Arona a section of wall was blown into the air, only for it to fall back into its foundations so neatly 'that the besieged were none the worse off'. And it was well known that artillery tactics could often backfire. James II of Scotland was killed when one of his own cannon exploded. Loose sparks could ignite one's powder keg or even those of your fellow men. And during the bungled assassination of the Prince of Orange in 1582, the assassin lost his thumb when his over-charged pistol blew up, allowing him to be apprehended and killed. Against Machiavelli, Montaigne recognizes that in this new age of weaponry, 'Events and consequences, especially in war, depend mostly on fortune' (a word whose ubiquity in the *Essays* got Montaigne into trouble with the Papal censor with its suggestions of a limit to divine providence). Even our 'reason and foresight', 'our counsels and calculations' – i.e. our supposed *virtù* – are not exempt, being themselves made up of 'a large element of chance'.

But with this sense of randomness, the link between morality and military success also comes unstuck, and as a result Montaigne begins to address a different set of questions. In 'By Diverse Means We Arrive at the Same End', he therefore poses a dilemma that would confound even Machiavelli. What do we do when we find ourselves at the mercy of a conquering force – i.e. what do we do when all our attempts to outwit fortune have *failed*? And here he recognizes that in favouring the brave, fortune persecutes others. He asks whether it is therefore sometimes better to run away than stoically stand our ground and writes essays on fear and on cowardice, certainly the most common but least discussed aspects of war. He tells how the twelfth-century King of Navarre quivered so much before going into battle that he became known as 'Garcia the Trembler'.

This is not to say that Montaigne does not retain a certain affection for the military life. He praises it for its variety and camaraderie:

> There is a pleasure in the company of so many men – noble, young, active men . . . in the liberty of that artless conversation, in a manly way of life without ceremony, in the variety of a thousand diverse actions, in this

courageous harmony of military music which warms and excites the ears and the soul . . . Company supplies confidence even to children.

But with the first salvos of the artillery, this bonhomie is shattered, and Montaigne appreciates the lonely terror of the modern soldier, pitted against his equally terrified opponent:

Him you see scrambling up the ruins of that wall, frantic and beside himself, the target of so many arquebus shots; and the other, scarred all over, weak and pale with hunger, and yet determined to die rather than to open the gates to him; do you think that they are there for themselves? No, rather on the behalf of one who they've never seen and who has no concern for their fate . . .

Having witnessed military action, Montaigne understands the arbitrary barbarity of modern war: men 'hacked and hewed to pieces . . . suffering a bullet to be pulled out from amongst their shattered bones'. Men screaming at the 'cauterizing and probing of wounds'. Not surprisingly, he confesses to jumping out of his skin when the 'rattle of an arquebus thunders in my ears all of a sudden, and in a place where I least expect it' – something that may give his fellow soldiers 'something to laugh at', but also comes at a human cost: the loss of a 'beloved brother' killed not from want of valour but simply by 'an unlucky bullet'. For Montaigne, the enemy is not simply one's opponent, but the indiscriminate randomness of war, overseen not by the breastplated Mars, but by Fortune, her eyes smarting in a cloud of gunsmoke, and whose 'lightning and thunder of . . . cannon and arquebuses', he remarks, 'are enough to frighten Caesar himself'.

On 22 August 1572, shortly after attending the marriage of Margaret de Valois and Henri de Navarre, the Protestant leader Gaspard de Coligny was walking down the street when he bent over to attend to his shoelaces. At that moment an arquebus shot tore off the index finger of his right hand whilst another ripped through his left arm, shattering his elbow. His would-be assassin, firing from a window overlooking the street, had missed his mark, and what was intended as a self-contained 'hit' ricocheted with disastrous consequences.

The marriage had been arranged as a desperate attempt to heal the dynastic and religious divisions of the time (Margaret was Charles IX's sister), but with Coligny injured, the Huguenot (i.e. Protestant) leadership chose to stay in Paris rather than fleeing, leading to fears of an imminent Huguenot revolt. And at a midnight meeting in the Louvre on the night of the 23rd, Charles decided to have the Huguenot leadership slain – including Coligny as he lay being tended in his bed. The slaughter of Protestants that followed – what became known as the St Bartholomew's Day Massacre – spread as far as Toulouse, Rouen and Bordeaux, killing around 10,000 Protestants and giving the world a new word, '*massacre*', from the old French for butchery, a word that Montaigne adds to the final edition of his text.

It was the most notorious incident in the French Wars of Religion which stretched from 1562 to 1598, and over half of Montaigne's adult lifetime – a period in which he described his country as a 'disturbed and sick state'. For now war was a religious matter, fought within countries, not between them, dividing towns, streets and houses; a conflict not unlike the break-up of the former Yugoslavia in our own time. In his own region of Gascony, Bordeaux was staunchly Catholic, yet Bergerac, upstream on the Dordogne, was a Protestant stronghold, known as the Geneva of France. Montaigne was stranded between the two.

The source of this religious violence was the Reformation's challenge to the Catholic Church's dominance of the Christian West. Martin Luther had upset the apple-cart of religion in the 1520s with his defiance of the Pope over the selling of indulgences. But now the apples accelerated dangerously downhill, tipping France into what the eighteenth-century historian and statesman Pierre Daunou called 'the most tragic century in all history'.

The theological roots of the conflict lay in the Reformers' extension of humanist techniques of textual exegesis from the texts of antiquity to the scriptures themselves. Christian humanists such as Erasmus thought the Word of God had been smothered by centuries of scholastic commentary and needed to return to the source – *ad fontes* – the original utterances of Christianity, facilitated by new translations of the scriptures from the Hebrew and the Greek. The humanist goal of linguistic and moral improvement thus acquired a religious dimension, merging the goals of moral and spiritual perfection into one.

Reformers such as Luther went beyond this, however, insisting that with the invention of printing the Bible should be translated from Latin into the vernacular and made the self-justifying centre of Christianity – *sola scriptura*. The plural noun of the scriptures – which were scattered around in various versions – became fused into the singular noun of the Bible (literally, the book). And the difficulty and obscurity of the biblical text – which the Church had used previously to justify its restricted circulation – became for Luther an exercise in spiritual enlightenment, as one passed from the letter into the spirit of the Word of God: from biblical illiteracy to illumination. A new, vernacular form of religiosity emerged, taking the Bible, rather than the priest, as its focus and brooding on the injustice of Papal rule from Rome.

What added to the divisiveness of reform, however, especially in France, was the higher-tuning given to Luther's message by John Calvin. Luther had argued for the reform of those practices unjustified by the Bible, and exploited by Rome, such as the selling of indulgences. Yet his theology was not entirely divorced from traditional Catholic practice: he did not object to the use of images or music in church and thought that the body of Christ was somehow still present in the Eucharist.

But Calvin's theology was characterized by a more strident mindset, no doubt influenced by his reading of the Stoics (his first published work was a commentary on Seneca). For Calvin, like the Stoics, virtue and vice did not mix, and nor did God's Word mix with the traditional practices of Catholicism. A highly theorized theological consciousness thus evolved that seemed to detect religious hypocrisy wherever it looked, Calvin asking in his commentary on Seneca:

> Are there not also in our own age, *monsters of men, dripping with inner vices*, yet putting forth the outward appearance and mask of uprightness? Yet *they shall melt like wax* when *truth, the daughter of time*, shall reveal herself. Let them sell as they will sad-faced shows of piety to the public, the time will come when *he who has sold smoke will perish by smoke*.

The Reformation thus became a battle over not simply religious power, but the basic criteria of religious truth. And in doing so it anticipated and exacerbated the inbuilt sectarianism of sixteenth-century French politics. The lines of religious intolerance were being laid down; it required only the divergent ambitions of differing political factions to provide the spark.

The tinderbox for these theological differences was provided by the jostling of various competing aristocratic alliances. Protestants allied themselves to the Bourbon line, led by Henri de Navarre, his cousin, Henri Prince of Condé, and Gaspard de Coligny, of the Châtillon family. The Catholic forces were led by the Guise family, led by Henri de Guise who oversaw the execution of Coligny and his uncle the Cardinal of Lorraine. Attempting, and spectacularly failing, to keep the peace between these competing interests was the royal family, its power fatally weakened by the accidental death of Henry II, who had been speared through the visor of his helmet by a broken lance during a tournament in 1559. His sons were minors, and France was ruled by a regency council headed by their mother, Catherine de' Medici.

In 1551 Sebastien Castellio – an early proponent of freedom of conscience – saw the storm coming, and in his dedication of his French Bible to Henry II described a darkness that was becoming all too visible:

> When night falls upon the battlefield, the combatants wait for the day lest by chance friends be killed instead of enemies, for it is better to spare one's enemies than to kill some of one's friends. Likewise, also in the daytime, when the hand-to-hand combat begins, the artillery ceases for fear of the aforesaid mischance. Here I should like to point a moral,

if Your Majesty will listen. The world today is embroiled in a great disturbance principally touching the question of religion. There never were so many calamities and evils, from which we may well perceive the night of ignorance . . . if it were day there would never be such diverse and even contrary judgements about the same colour. Or if it is day, at least the good and evil are so confused in the matter of religion that if one wishes to disentangle those who are at variance as to the truth there is danger lest the wheat be rooted out with the tares . . . Believe me, Your Majesty, the world today is neither better nor wiser nor more enlightened than formerly. It were better, therefore, in view of so much doubt and confusion to wait before shooting until dawn or until things are better disentangled, lest in the darkness and confusion we do that of which afterward we shall have to say, 'I did not intend to.'

Castellio's patient liberalism was fatally out of sympathy with the times, however. He was persecuted by Calvin and died ostracized and poor. And in 1562, after a massacre of Protestants at Vassey in Champagne, civil war broke out in France, bringing with it exactly the night of ignorance that Castellio had foreseen.

The earliest surviving letter we have from Montaigne comes from the same year, when he writes to Antoine Duprat, the provost of Paris, telling him of the religious violence that has broken out in the region. He tells him of Monluc's brutal suppression of the Huguenot forces around Agen, where 'every kind of cruelty and violence was practised . . . without regard to status, sex, or age'. But then Montaigne comes to the real reason he has written:

It is with extreme sorrow that I tell you that also involved in this massacre was your relative, the wife of Gaspard Duprat, and two of her children. She was a noble woman, whom I have often had the opportunity of seeing when I was in those parts, and at whose house I was always assured of receiving hospitality. In short, I say no more to you about it today, for this account gives me pain and sorrow . . .

In the midst of this spiralling violence Montaigne remained loyal to the King, but he also attempted to negotiate between the warring factions, and became close to Henri de Navarre, the leader of the Protestant cause. But his task was made difficult by the fractious conditions of civil war, where the distinction between principle and private interest was never clear.

For what seemed shocking about the French civil wars was the idea that the normal rules of conflict seemed to have been suspended. The Middle Ages had seen the elaboration of an idea of 'just' war, fought to retrieve land or property, or simply to oppose evil with good − and here the Crusades provided ample opportunities for do-gooding. Furthermore, the cult of chivalry cast warfare within a noble, Christian light. But during the French Wars of Religion the violence seemed to spill out beyond these conventions. Rumour and conspiracy were rife and, most dangerously, an equal, Christian legitimacy was asserted by both sides. The fierce violence released by this cocktail of dynastic rivalries, spiked with religious zeal, was truly horrific. 'Monstrous war', Montaigne exclaims: 'Other wars act outwardly, this one acts against itself, eating away and destroying itself with its own venom.'

And one symptom of this was a prevailing sense of uncertainty about the difference between friend and foe. The fighting was particularly bad in Montaigne's region, where Henri de Navarre had most of his support. And Montaigne gives a vivid picture of the ugly and suspicious times in which he lived:

> Travelling together one day during the Civil Wars, my brother the Sieur de la Brousse and I met a gentleman of good sort. He was of the opposite party to ourselves, although I knew nothing of it, for he pretended otherwise; and the evil of these wars is that the cards are so shuffled, your enemy not being distinguished from yourself by any apparent mark, either of language or appearance, and nourished under the same laws, customs, and the same air, so that it is very hard to avoid confusion and disorder. This made me myself afraid of meeting any of our own troops in a place where I was not known, in case I was not able to reveal my name . . . As had happened to me before, where, by such mischance, I lost both men and horses, and most tragically, a page, an Italian gentleman, whom I had brought up with the greatest care: in which a life of great promise and expectation was extinguished.

Civil war thus results in not only a breakdown of society but a breakdown of trust – Montaigne fearing his own side almost as much as his enemy. Whereas in a foreign campaign one is fighting strangers, civil wars require the deliberate estrangement of parties that may already know each other: 'they make us stand guard in our own houses'; 'your own servant may be on the side you fear'. Montaigne's earliest essays vividly capture this tragic breakdown. He relates how at Mussidan, only seventeen miles from Montaigne, he saw the inhabitants slaughtered whilst peace negotiations were still going on. He tells how he has gone to bed a thousand times fearing that he would be slaughtered that very night and has to fend off an attempt by one of his neighbours to seize his house. He records the pitiful fate of a tailor across the river in St Foy-la-Grande, killed with sixty stabs of his own scissors 'for twenty sous and a coat'.

The innate randomness of modern artillery warfare is thus exacerbated by the hypocrisy of the motives for which it is fought:

> Our zeal performs wonders when it seconds our inclinations to hatred, cruelty, ambition, avarice, detraction, rebellion. But moved . . . towards goodness, benignity, moderation, unless by miracle some rare disposition prompt us to it, we stir neither hand nor foot. Our religion is intended to eradicate vices whereas it covers, nourishes, incites them.

He pictures soldiers, saying their prayers before mounting an attack, but with their 'desires full of cruelty, avarice, and lust'. Seeing the civil wars of his time, he asks, 'Who does not cry out that the machine of the world is in dissolution and that the end of the world is at hand?'

For Montaigne, himself a member of the nobility of the sword, the noblest profession thus reveals the caprices of fortune: the stratagems of military planners maliciously unwound by ill-luck. Moreover, the natural bonds between people are severed by civil war – the 'divisions and subdivisions' which threaten to tear his country apart – rendering them incapable and indeed scornful of sympathy and fellow feeling. Human behaviour, like that of gunpowder, is now unpredictable: we wander a battlefield in darkness and despair.

Do you jump or duck at the bang of an arquebus? Do you defy or prostrate yourself before your enemy? There is no way of knowing: 'We have no grip on what is to come.' The one thing that you do know is that you will die; and the only thing you have control over – on the arbitrary battlefield of sixteenth-century France – is how well you prepare yourself for that fact.

4

To Philosophize Is to Learn to Die

In a series of woodcuts entitled *The Dance of Death* of 1543, Hans Holbein pictures Death skipping through the miseries of early modern Europe like a grimly nimble Fred Astaire. He pavanes with popes, gambols with gamblers, sarabands with sailors, but in one truly awful image he leads away a young boy as his mother sits cooking in their poor poverty-stricken home. All of Holbein's unflinching brilliance is evident here. The young boy reaching back to his mother. The mother beside herself, clutching at her hair. And Death himself, with his dapper gait and cheesy grin – already out of the door.

In the sixteenth century death seemed to be on the offensive: Montaigne quotes Seneca on the fact that 'death is everywhere', and Holbein goes on to depict Death's jaunty vitality as he shins up and snaps the masts of sailing ships and drinks drunkards under the ground. Moreover, the reasons for his cheerfulness are not difficult to discern. War ravaged the countryside. Illness and injury took their toll. Plague, syphilis, and typhus cut a swathe through the population, leaving death at once both terrifying and terrifyingly familiar. At Ames near Lille in 1580, a young man named Jehan le Porcq died of a contagious illness, spending his final days in a shed at the bottom of his father's garden.

Moreover, a new sense of spiritual uncertainty seemed to have undermined the traditional solace offered by the Church. The historian Philippe Ariès describes the medieval period as operating with a notion of 'tamed death', in which death was merely a station in a spiritual narrative that stretched from the present through to the everafter. But after the Reformation this story seems to have become interrupted; our salvation was no longer secure: and Death sat up in all his awful wonder. Looking closely at Holbein's woodcut we can glimpse a sense of this harrowing uncertainty, as the wisps of smoke begin to cloud and smother the boy's hand as he is dragged from this life into the unknown.

In his first book of essays, Montaigne thus sees death as the overwhelming moral, theological, and philosophical problem that we face: 'All the wisdom and reasoning in this world finally boils down to one point: to teach us not to be afraid to die.' He constantly, obsessively returns to it. It is his inspiration for writing – so that his 'relatives and friends' may remember him 'when they have lost me (as soon they must)'. And it is the one essential, central task of philosophy – as he declares in the title of one of his earliest compositions: 'To Philosophize Is to Learn to Die'.

❧

Montaigne's world was a violent one in which wars, jousts, duels and executions were a common spectacle, where life, in Hobbes's words, was 'nasty, brutish, and short'. As Montaigne strolled as a tourist through the streets of Rome in January 1581 he came upon the execution of an infamous bandit, Catena, who had killed a pair of Capuchin monks, forcing them to abjure God before cutting their throats. As the murderer was paraded through the streets, two monks preached at him, whilst another pressed a portrait of Jesus into his face:

> At the gallows, which is a beam between two supports, they kept this picture against his face until he was given the drop. He made an ordinary death, without movement

or word. He was a dark man about thirty or thereabouts. After he was strangled, they cut him into four quarters.

It was an 'ordinary death', observes Montaigne, and goes on to note that the spectators only cried out when he began to be cut up.

How many ways has death to surprise us? asks Montaigne. Who would have thought a Duke of Brittany would have been crushed to death as he led the Pope's horse through a crowd; that Henry II of France would die when a splinter pierced his eye during a playful joust; that the son of Louis VI would be killed by an angry hog. That Aeschylus would make his final exit when a vulture dropped a tortoise on his stone-like bald head. One dies choking on a grape; another scratching himself with a comb; the Roman Aufidius walked into a door. And Montaigne describes the numbers of men who have perished trying redress the balance – between women's thighs, as he puts it: Ludovico, the son of the Marquis of Mantua; Plato's nephew, the philosopher Speusippus; even a Pope! From this final enemy, as Propertius says, no helmet can defend you: 'Death will eventually drag forth your head.'

And turning to his own family, Montaigne records the tragic fate of his younger brother Arnaud, killed during a game of tennis:

> And if I may intrude myself, a brother of mine, Captain Saint Martin, at the age twenty years, who had already given sufficient proof of his valour, whilst playing tennis received a blow from a ball a little above his right ear, without any apparent wound or bleeding. He did not sit down or rest, but five or six hours later died of an apoplexy caused by the blow. With such frequent and

common examples passing before our eyes, how is it possible to disengage oneself from thinking of death, and that at each moment it has us by the throat?

As he begins writing his essays at the age of thirty-nine, Montaigne therefore feels that he is living on borrowed time. Average life expectancy during the period was around thirty-three years; Etienne de La Boétie died at thirty-two. And so as he finishes his thirties, Montaigne sees himself as embarked upon a process of inevitable and increasingly precipitous decline:

> Poor fool that you are, who has assured you of the term of your life? You are relying on physicians' stories. Look at facts and experience. By the common course of things, you have already lived by extraordinary favour. You have already passed the normal limits of life. And to prove it, count up your acquaintances; how many have died before your age than have attained it; and of those who have distinguished their lives by their renown, make a list, and I'll wager you will find more who have died before than after thirty-five years of age.

'To die of old age,' he concludes, 'is a death rare, singular and extraordinary, and therefore, the most unnatural.'

And as if to seal this despondency, Montaigne recognizes the fact that childbirth only too often served to deliver death into the world. During the sixteenth century around half of all children died in infancy, often from simple infections (and being sent out to nurse, as Montaigne's children were, only served to make them more susceptible). In his copy of Beuther's *Ephemeris Historia*, Montaigne thus records the heartbreak of his first-born daughter, born after four years of trying:

1570. June 28. Born of Françoise de La Chassaigne and myself a daughter that my mother and Monsieur the President de La Chassaigne, father of my wife, named Thoinette. She was the first child of our marriage, and died two months later.

Over the next thirteen years he records the death of four others: Anne, born 5 July 1573 and who died seven weeks later. Another nameless daughter born 27 December 1574 and who lasted only three months. Another daughter, again unnamed, was born and died on 16 May 1577. And finally Marie, born 21 February 1583, who lived for only a few days. Only Léonor, born 9 September 1571, survived into adulthood. Montaigne concludes, with an air of understandable bitterness: 'all of mine die in infancy'.

In his *Alphabet of Death* of 1538 Holbein shows Death stealing a baby from its cot. Death's posture suggests a chilling playfulness. But the baby looks out at us in an expression of almost rebuke in the terrifying blankness of its stare. The accompanying text is taken from Job 14, 1–2: 'Man that is born of a woman is of few days, and full of trouble. He cometh forth like a flower, and is cut down: he fleeth also as a shadow, and continueth not.'

❧

Montaigne's response to this gloomy pessimism – as it was for every right-thinking man at the time – was to go on the offensive, and take on Death, man to man: 'Let us learn to stand our ground and fight.' And Montaigne's most crucial weapon in this is what he refers to at one point as 'the leading and most authoritative philosophy' of the ancients: Stoicism – the writings of Seneca, Epictetus, and the emperor Marcus Aurelius; a moral fibre that wound its way through the theological and philosophical fabric of the West. It was this that had consoled La Boétie on his deathbed, and so it would do for Montaigne.

Stoicism took its name from the Stoa, or porch, where the first of the Stoics, the Greek philosopher Zeno, instructed his disciples. Originally, it comprised a system of metaphysics, logic, and ethics, but it was as an ethical theory that it found its most influential fruition in the Roman republic in the first century CE. At its heart Stoicism was a programme for dealing with misfortune – illness, military defeat, and death – teaching that the goal of philosophy was a cultivated indifference to such misery (in this Epictetus, who was lamed by a cruel master, and Seneca, who was to commit suicide after falling foul of Nero, seemed to know what they were talking about). Stoicism therefore advised that one should separate one's reason from the passions and the senses, thereby achieving a state of *apatheia* (impassivity) and therefore *constantia* (constancy), which allowed one to face trials and tribulations with a stiff upper lip (Zeno pictured the soul of the Stoic sage as a tightly clenched fist). By following these prescriptions the Stoic sage was thus able to rise above the devastating effects of emotional ties, such as family – as Epictetus advised:

> As on a voyage when the vessel has reached a port, if you go out to get water, it is an amusement on the way to pick up a seashell or some bulb, but your thoughts ought to be directed to the ship, and you ought to be constantly watching if the captain should call, and then you must throw away all those things . . . so in life also, if there be given to you instead of a little bulb and a seashell, a wife and child, there will be nothing to prevent you from taking them. But if the captain should call, run to the ship, and leave all those things without regard to them . . .
>
> If you love an earthen jug, say it is an earthen jug which you love; for when it has been broken, you will not be disturbed. If you are kissing your child or wife, say that it is a human being whom you are kissing, for when the wife or child dies, you will not be disturbed.

Stoicism was thus supposed to offer philosophical solace in times of grief, but to the martial, duty-bound Roman republic it also amounted to a powerful ideological creed. Montaigne tells the story of Gaius Mucius Scaevola, who, after being captured and threatened with torture by the Etruscans, thrust his fist into a brazier without flinching, causing them to gulp at this example of Roman fortitude and surrender there and then.

During the Middle Ages, this Stoic attitude became absorbed into Christianity, which shared its hair-shirted seriousness and worldly contempt, as can be seen in

Boethius's *Consolations of Philosophy*. But during the sixteenth century Stoicism seemed to undergo a revival, partly as a result of humanists' enthusiasm for antiquity (such as was shown by Erasmus, who edited Seneca), but also because of the role it played in formulating the Protestant Reformation, where humanistically trained reformers rebundled Stoic fortitude into a new, militant form of faith. But with the hardening of religious attitudes that inevitably resulted, Stoicism began to snowball, almost in a kind of ideological feedback loop. For what made it so difficult to displace as an attitude was the fact that it was seen to be quintessentially noble, honourable – *male* – and no self-respecting sixteenth-century man who called himself a man would beg to differ, as is affirmed in an emblem from Henry Peacham's *Minerva Britannica* (1612):

Amid the waves, a mightie Rock doth stand,
Whose ruggie brow, had bidden many a shower,
And bitter storme; which neither sea, nor land,
Nor JOVES sharpe-lightening ever could devoure:
This same is MANLIE CONSTANCIE of mind,
Not easly moov'd with every blast of wind.

Other writers refined this neo-Stoic synthesis of classical and Christian ideas, such as the Dutch humanist Justus Lipsius in his *De Constantia* (1584), and the French statesman Guillaume du Vair in his *De la Constance* of 1594. But perhaps the most influential transformation of the Stoic ethos comes in the work of the early seventeenth-century philosopher René Descartes.

Descartes is often referred to as the 'father of modern philosophy', the first to place philosophy on something like a scientific footing. But his thinking can also be seen as a response to a breakdown in society similar to Montaigne's, in his case the context of the wider European conflict of the Thirty Years War. What Descartes sets out to do is to effectively distance his mind from his body and achieve a more thoroughgoing stoical *apatheia* as a result. He thus describes himself at the beginning of his *Discourse on Method* as finding himself in Neuburg, a peaceful Catholic principality on the Danube, where he feels 'undisturbed by any passions or cares' – a stoical stance he repeats in the French version of his *Meditations* of 1647:

Now, then, that I have opportunely freed my mind from all cares and am happily disturbed by no passions, and since I am in the secure possession of leisure in a peaceable solitude, I shall at last apply myself earnestly and freely to the general overthrow of all my ancient opinions.

In his *Discourse on Method* he vows to follow his own intellectual 'rules' with a 'firm and constant resolution' ('une ferme et constante résolution'), vowing 'to be as firm and resolute in my actions as I could' ('le plus ferme et le plus résolu en mes actions que je pourrois'), and to follow even doubtful opinions 'with no less constancy' ('ne suivre pas moins constamment') – like a lost traveller who resolves to keep walking in a straight line.

But in order to find a *truly* 'constant' – i.e. certain – position, Descartes makes a new departure. For rather than resisting 'falsehood' or 'opinion', through fortitude, Descartes chooses to embrace them and raise doubts that are so extreme that they can *only* be imagined – that an evil spirit may be deceiving him; 'that sky, air, earth, colours, shapes, sounds . . . are mere delusive dreams'. But the payback of this speculation is that thought emerges as the one constant, as without *thinking* such impossible notions could not take place:

> . . . I noticed that, whilst I wished to think that all was false, it was necessary that I who was thinking had to be something; and noting that this truth, 'I think, therefore I am,' was so firm and so assured, that all the most extravagant suppositions of the sceptics were not capable of shaking it.

What is clear is that it is the idea of a Stoic 'core' that prepares the ground for the Cartesian *cogito*, a thinking subject impervious not simply to misfortune but also to doubt. And the centrality of this Stoic separation of the mind from the body to Descartes' thought is suggested by the long title of his magnum opus: *Meditations on First Philosophy in which are demonstrated the existence of God and the distinction between the human soul and the body.*

Descartes is thus correctly described as the 'father' of modern philosophy; but he can also be said to represent a culmination: the final transformation of neo-Stoic ethics into a neo-Stoic epistemology, where thought is absolutely distanced from its embodiment; where constancy and incorrigibility coincide.

~

In his earliest essays, Montaigne displays a similarly Stoic bravado in facing up to death: 'let us stiffen and fortify ourselves'; 'let us look for it [death] everywhere'; 'the end of our race is death; it is the necessary object of our aim, which, if it frights us, how is it possible to take a step without feverishness?' All the actions of our life should be directed towards this final showdown: 'In this last scene there is no counterfeiting: we must speak out plain and display what there is that is good and clean at the bottom of the pot.'

And into this stoical pessimism Montaigne mixes Lucretius' cosmological atomism, where life is passed on like a baton in an endless relay race: 'Your death is part of the order of the universe, it is part of the life of the world'. Why, therefore, 'seek to add longer life, merely to renew ill-spent time and be tormented?' For, as Montaigne comments:

> . . . if you have lived one day, you have seen them all. One day is equal to all other days. There is no other light, no other shade. This sun, this moon, these stars, this disposition of things is the same your ancestors enjoyed, and will also entertain your descendants.

Why drag things out? 'We are turning in the same circle,' says Lucretius, 'ever confined therein.' There are no new things to please you: 'It is the same over and over again.' The true task of life is, therefore, 'to lay a foundation for death'.

True to his word, Montaigne recalls how, even in his youth, morbid thoughts would strike him in the most unlikely situations: 'in the company of ladies and at games'. And he tells how someone turning over some of his papers came across a note he had written about something he wished to be done after his death, a note he had written down whilst less than a mile from his house, whilst perfectly healthy but still unsure whether he would survive the journey home. Whereas others may complain that death surprises them and breaks off their plans – the education of their children, their daughter's marriage – Montaigne insists we should be always be at the ready: 'We should be booted and ready to go.'

❧

Montaigne's Stoic pessimism comes to a head in his essay 'Of Practice', in which he looks back to the late 1560s to an incident when he was knocked off his horse and almost killed. The essay addresses the paradox that death is 'the greatest task we have to perform' and yet the one thing for which we cannot rehearse: 'Practice can give us no assistance . . . we are all apprentices when we come to it.' Hence his interest in his own near-death experience:

> During our third or second civil wars (I do not well remember which), I went out one day, about a league from my house, which is seated in the middle of all the trouble of the civil wars in France. Thinking myself safe as I was so near to my home that that there was no need

for a better mount, I had taken a very easy but not very strong horse. On my return . . . one of my men, a tall, strong fellow, mounted upon a strong packhorse that had a very hard mouth [i.e. was obstinate] and was fresh and vigorous, to play the brave and get ahead of his fellows, came at full speed down my track, and crashed like a thunderbolt into the little man and little horse, striking us with such strength and weight, that he sent us both head over heels into the air. So that there lay the horse overthrown and stunned with the fall, I ten or twelve paces further away, dead, stretched out, with my face all battered and broken, my sword which I had had in my hand, more than ten paces away, and my belt all broken to pieces, with no more life or feeling than a log.

His men gather round and try to revive him but, failing to rouse him, fear the worst and begin to carry his body back to his house. But on the way he begins to cough and throw up blood, only to lapse back into unconsciousness, to the extent that 'my first sentiments were much nearer to death than to life'. Word of the accident reaches his home and his wife and daughter rush out to meet him. He hears their voices, but only at the periphery of his soul. He fumbles with his doublet. He sees his wife stumbling and in his delirium calls for someone to fetch her a horse. He quotes Tasso to the effect that his soul was clearly doubtful of ever returning to his body, having lost confidence in its link to life.

Montaigne's accident has all the signs of a serious concussion, the obvious consequences of which can be a stroke and, of course, death. But what is remarkable about his account is the fact that the prospect of death does not seem to disturb him. He says that his 'first thought was that I had been shot in the head with an arquebus, for indeed several were being fired around us at the time'. In other words, he has succumbed to the worse death imaginable, a random mixture of negligence and bad luck. Moreover, it has happened not on the field of battle, but on a path less than a mile from his house.

But as he lies there, unmoving upon the cold earth, it is Stoicism that comes to his aid. As he says, he tells this account in order to 'give us more fortitude' in the face of 'the greatest task we have to perform'. For what Montaigne seems to achieve in his final moments is exactly the state of *apatheia* that the Stoics cherished, declaring, with Holbein's *Ambassadors*, that this life is worth less than the next – or as La Boétie whispered on his deathbed: '*An vivere tanti est?*' (Is life worth so much?). In his late thirties, living, as he thinks, already on borrowed time; with his country in the midst of a violent civil war; with the deaths of fathers, brothers and friends all around him; with his face battered and broken, his sword ripped out of his hand, and with own extinction only fingertips away, Montaigne concludes, with Lucretius: *Nec nova vivendo procuditur ulla voluptas* – There is nothing to be gained by desperately hanging on to life – and gives up:

> I saw myself all covered in blood, for my doublet was stained all over with the blood I had vomited ... I thought my life was just hanging on the end of my lips, and I shut my eyes, to help, as I thought, to push it out, and took pleasure in languishing and letting myself go ...

5

Que sçais-je? – What Do I Know?

Around this time a fog descended over northern Europe. It covered the Rhine, merging with the reed beds and sea mists. It cloistered the churchyards of France. It slipped inside books, it tarnished sword blades. It scaled the high walls of Oxford and surrounded Aristotle. It seemed to enter flesh itself, and confuse the identities of things and the very boundaries of matter. And then it settled in men's minds.

Montaigne survived the fall from his horse. He was carried back to his house, coughing and retching, and lay in bed for several days refusing any treatment, convinced, as he says, that he had been 'mortally wounded in the head'. But when he sets about retelling the story of his accident in his essay 'Of Practice' (written perhaps some eight years after the event), something begins to cloud his Stoic resolution – not fear or cowardice, but a new sense of the doubtfulness and uncertainty of our knowledge, a new sense of the sceptical fog in which we are immersed.

Scepticism arrived as a new and intoxicating intellectual force in the sixteenth century. Again it was an idea that had ancient precedents, particularly in the writings of the Greek sceptic Sextus Empiricus, whose *Outlines of Pyrrhonism* Montaigne knew from the translation of Henri Estienne of 1562. But as well as communicating these ancient ideas, the 'revival' of scepticism seemed to bespeak a loss of intellectual confidence more generally, no doubt as a result of the turmoil brought in by the Reformation, an uncertainty reflected in the title of Francisco Sanchez's *Quod nihil scitur* (*That Nothing Is Known*), published within a year of Montaigne's *Essays* in 1581.

For, as Montaigne describes the aftermath of his fall he thus seems to become strangely enthralled by the sceptical wonder of his near-death experience, and the strange confusion caused by his knock on the head:

> . . . the fact is I was not there at all: these were but idle thoughts, in the clouds, stirred up by the senses of the eyes and ears, and not coming from me. I did not know where I had come from or where I was going; nor was I able to weigh and consider what I was asked: these were light effects, that the senses produced of themselves out of habit. What the soul contributed was in a dream, lightly touched, licked and moistened by the soft impression of the senses.

More vividly than any abstract argument, Montaigne's accident thus shows him that our minds are closely related to the body: 'the functions of the soul . . . regained life at the same rate as those of the body'. Moreover, the body may, in fact, be more capable on its own: he only began to 'move and to breathe', he recalls, because 'so great a quantity of blood had fallen into my stomach that Nature needed to rouse her forces to discharge it'. By contrast his mind, his reason, is out for the count: the 'weakness' of his understanding depriving him of the 'faculty of discerning' what had happened. He concludes that in those who have suffered terrible injuries, 'their minds and bodies are submerged in sleep'.

So whilst Montaigne might have embarked on 'Of Practice' to prove a Stoic point – that we should not be afraid of death – as he begins to write it down an alternative interpretation starts to take shape. Firstly, he realizes that the mind *is* necessarily tied to the body, and as a consequence our ability to distance ourselves from our passions and our senses is necessarily curtailed. Our basic condition is one of grogginess and uncertainty; despite our pretensions to knowledge, we may be concussed in the first place – as he later declares:

> We wake sleeping, and in our waking sleep. I do not see so clearly in my sleep; but as to my waking, I never find it sufficiently clear and cloudless. Moreover, the deepest sleep sometimes puts dreams to sleep. But our waking is never so awake that it purges and dissipates those reveries which are the dreams of the waking, and worse than our dreams.

But the second implication – an idea that runs through the later essays like the underground streams nourishing the vines around him – is that the vulnerability of our consciousness suggests the vulnerability of our souls. He says that it was impossible that his soul 'could maintain any force within to recognize itself'. Our final moments – from the perspective of one who has 'essayed' them – reveal not the imperiousness and composure of the soul, but its confusion, its concussion, and its likely dissolution as a result. And this has clear theological implications – in bringing Montaigne to the boundaries of atheism – but philosophical implications as well: for if we possess no umbilical link to the afterlife (and hence to God), our ability to reach perfect knowledge is also jeopardized. We are effectively on our own.

Montaigne's fall from his horse, 'so light an incident', is therefore an experience that stays with him for the rest of his life: 'To this moment I still feel the bruises of that terrible shock.' But it also becomes a momentous event in terms of the redirection of human knowledge that it suggests: away from a

Christian humanist yearning for the afterlife, and back to the human, to the body, to the *natural*. And when he returns to 'Of Practice' in his final additions to the essays – additions that are characterized by their honesty and intellectual courage – it is this rudderless yet intoxicating freedom that Montaigne emphasizes, seeing the process of self-analysis as something radically new – a 'new and extraordinary undertaking':

> And should it be taken amiss if I communicate it. What is of use to me, may perhaps be of use to another. As to the rest, I am not hurting anything; I use nothing but that which is my own. And if I play the fool, it is at my own expense, and nobody else's business. For it is a folly that will die with me, and has no consequence. We have only heard of two or three of the ancients who have beaten this path, and yet I cannot say if it was in a similar manner, knowing nothing of them but their names. No one since has followed this track. It is a difficult undertaking, more difficult than it seems, to follow a gait so rambling and uncertain as that of the mind; to penetrate the dark profundities of its inner windings; to identify and lay hold of all the delicate airs of its motions. It is a new and extraordinary undertaking, and which withdraws us from the common and most recommended employments of the world.

The 'two or three ancients' that Montaigne refers to could be any number of figures, but a strong possibility is the pre-Socratic materialists, Leucippus, Democritus and Epicurus, who were often described as constituting a 'school' of atheism (hence, perhaps, Montaigne's unwillingness to name them), and whose writings no longer exist, their views only coming down to us second-hand. As a consequence, the soul/self is not something that is simply assumed, but something whose nature is to be actively discovered. Rather than the soul trying to escape its embodiment, it should embrace it, explore it. The 'vanity' of such an activity goes against the Christian/Stoic consensus of his time ('the most recommended employments of the world'). But it is, he insists, sticking to his guns: 'a folly that will die with me'.

Montaigne thus begins to forge a bridge between his preoccupation with death – and Stoicism as an antidote to that fear of death – to the more sceptical outlook displayed in the essays that Montaigne composes in the mid-1570s, where 'both within and without, man is full of weakness and falsehood'. But with it comes a distancing from the stoical infatuations of his youth, the cult of death that had tied him to the memory of La Boétie.

For at some point Montaigne decides to no longer live under the baleful influence of Lucretius' philosophical pessimism, and reaches up to erase it from his ceiling, leaving only the barest of outlines –

– and replaces it with the humbler wisdom of the book of Ecclesiastes: SICVT IGNORAS QVOMODO ANIMA CONIVNGATVR CORPORI SIC NESCIS OPERA DEI / You who do not know how the mind is joined to the body know nothing of the works of God.

Echoing it on other joists, he records other sceptical statements, in a cosmic mind map that reaches from Euripides and Ecclesiastes, to Pliny and St Paul:

And who knows if this thing, which is called life,
is death, whilst to live is to die?

Man is clay

The only thing certain is that nothing is certain
and nothing is more wretched or proud than man

Emptiness everywhere

And on the main beams of his ceiling, more weightily profound that the rest, he inscribes the prudent scepticism of Sextus:

With wavering judgement
I do not understand
Nothing to a greater extent than the other
Inclining to neither side
I do not grasp
I attend to
I consider
With custom as sense and guide

Montaigne's most sustained engagement with scepticism, however, comes in his essay 'An Apology for Raymond Sebond', prompted by the work of the fifteenth-century Spanish theologian that he had translated at his father's request – a story that he tells at the start of the essay. His father had made his house open to men of learning during the flourishing of humanism at the time of Francis I, and one of them, Pierre Bunel, presented his father with Sebond's *Natural Theology, or Book of the Creatures*, presenting it as an antidote to the 'novel doctrines of Luther' which were then coming into vogue.

Sebond's book lay under a 'pile of neglected papers' for many years until Montaigne's father came across it a few days before his death, and asked his eldest son to put it into French, which he did; he was 'singularly pleased with it' and gave instructions to have it published. It is this book, printed in Paris in 1569, that Montaigne reflects upon in his 'Apology for Raymond Sebond', by far the longest of his essays. Here he outlines a sceptical, tolerant philosophy, summed up in the phrase '*Que sçais-je?*' (What do I know?), a phrase he says that he adopted as his personal motto, having it inscribed on a medal.

Montaigne's 'Apology' has become famous as the central statement of sixteenth-century scepticism, a critique of man's presumption and conceptual frailty. It builds on the keenly ironic sense of Montaigne's earlier essays, and the influence of his schooling, in the humanistic mode of argumentation *in utramque partem* – on either side of a case. But in the 'Apology' Montaigne expands his scepticism to defend Sebond.

Sebond had argued that God had provided man with two books – the scriptures and the natural world – in which he might 'read' proof of God's existence, where animals provide the alphabet, and man the initial capital letter. Sebond's arguments proved popular, sixteen editions being published after the second edition of 1485. But in the sixteenth century his work came under attack for its seeming privileging of nature over scripture, leading Pope Paul IV to place it on the Index of Forbidden Books in 1559.

Montaigne sets about defending his author against charges of heresy and simple-mindedness, first choosing to attack the intellectual arrogance of his detractors, declaring that 'presumption' is man's 'natural and original disease':

Who has persuaded him to believe that this wonderful

motion of the celestial vault, the eternal light of those torches that roll so proudly over his head, the dreadful movements of the boundless sea, were established, and endured so many ages, for his convenience and for his service? Is it possible to imagine anything so ridiculous as that this miserable and puny creature, who is not even master of himself, but exposed to blows from every angle, should call himself master and emperor of the universe, of which he has not the power to know the smallest part, much less to command it?

And against those who say that Sebond undervalues the role of faith, Montaigne does not find it difficult to point to the religious wars of his own time, and the hypocrisy of those who commit barbarous deeds in the name of theological 'purity':

And we think it strange if, in the wars which at this hour oppress our state, we see the issues bending and wavering in a common and ordinary manner. It is because we bring to them only that which is our own. The justice which is in one of the parties is there only for an ornament and covering . . . See the horrible impudence with which we bandy divine reasonings, and how irreligiously we have rejected and taken them up again, as fortune has changed our position in these public storms.

'There is no enmity excelling that of Christians,' he comments ruefully.

But Montaigne's 'Apology' has also given rise to the most discussion among commentators, basically in terms of what has been called the 'perplexing' contradiction between Sebond's belief that man can find theological support for his beliefs in the natural world and Montaigne's avowed scepticism – i.e.

his doubt about the power of reason. In what sense, therefore, can the essay be said to constitute an 'apology' or defence of Sebond?

If we look closely at the beginning of Montaigne's essay, however, we soon see that what Montaigne finds congenial in Sebond is not his belief in the power of reason in the abstract, but his belief that religion requires tactile, tangible support. It is Sebond's attempt to ground belief in 'human and natural reasons' with which Montaigne is most in sympathy – 'natural' for him being not a theoretical entity, but that which involves the body and our senses: 'to adapt to the service of our faith the natural and human instruments that God has endowed us':

> We do not content ourselves with serving God with our minds and souls; we also owe him a bodily reverence; we apply even our limbs and our movements and external things to honour him.

Religion is therefore something that we cannot help but understand in proximate terms – the feelings and sensations it arouses in us, its ties to our lands and customs, the sights and sounds of our local church. He writes of the island of Dioscorides (Soqotra in the Indian Ocean), where men are said to live happily as Christians, with rituals and feasts, but with no knowledge of the meaning of their religion at all. 'We are Christians,' Montaigne concludes, 'by the same title as we are Périgordians or Germans.'

And to prove the centrality of body and our senses to our being, Montaigne suggests a terrifying test for his Stoic, to see if he can think his way out of that:

> Let a philosopher be placed into a cage of thin iron bars, that is suspended from the top of a tower of Notre

Dame of Paris. He will see by evident reason that it is impossible to fall, and yet (unless he has been brought up as a steeplejack) he will not be able to avoid a feeling of terror and paralysis at the extreme height. For we have enough trouble reassuring ourselves in the galleries of our bell-towers if they are made with an open balustrade, even if it is made of stone. There are some who cannot even bear the thought of it. Let a plank be thrown between these two towers, of a width sufficient to walk upon. There is no philosophical wisdom of such firmness that it can give us the courage to walk on it, as we could if it were on the ground.

Whereas philosophers, in particular the Stoics, think they can escape the orbit of the body, Montaigne shows that ultimately, it is impossible: just as we find human intimacy comforting, great distances fill us with dread. The abstractions of theologians and philosophers fly in the face of even our instinct for self-preservation.

Scepticism thus arises from our attempt to escape our embodiment and raise hypotheses in areas where we have no grasp. And perhaps the clearest example of Montaigne's particular brand of scepticism is his attitude towards witchcraft, one of the most pressing intellectual topics of his age. In the two hundred years from 1450 to 1650 up to 100,000 people, mostly women, were tried as witches, and up to half of them executed as a result. One theory for the rise in prosecutions is that learned and legal opinion, traditionally sceptical, momentarily suspended its disbelief through an infatuation with demonology, thus releasing the floodgates of prejudice, misogyny and cruelty.

But here Montaigne, again, is remarkable for his intellectual independence. In his essay 'Of Cripples', in many ways a vehicle for his scepticism about witchcraft, he says that 'the witches in my neighbourhood are in danger for their lives when some new author appears whose opinion gives a body to their fancies.' He thus clearly sees the way traditional folk belief provided the raw material for demonological interpretation, and goes on to warn of the danger of using biblical sanction ('Thou shalt not suffer a witch to live') to support the deranged tales provided by witnesses, 'whether in giving evidence against another or against themselves'. That is to say, we should be mistrustful of confessions as much as accusations.

He gives the example of a prince who, in order 'to overcome my incredulity', showed him some ten or twelve witches that he held prisoner. They freely confessed their witchcraft, and had, the prince insisted, evidence of the devil's mark upon them. Montaigne was permitted to talk with them and ask as many questions as he wished, but concluded: 'In the end, in all conscience, I would rather have prescribed them hellebore [a cure for mental illness] than hemlock [a fatal poison].'

Montaigne's scepticism is thus opportunistic rather than schematic; less a dogmatic denial of knowledge (which itself smacks of presumption), and more a resistance to the inquisitorial mindset that characterized sixteenth-century intellectual life. The distinguished legal theorist Jean Bodin held that in cases of witchcraft even children could be tortured in order to reveal the elusive truths of the practice. Montaigne, by contrast, knows that such measures merely throw up more fictions:

> The rack is a dangerous invention, and moreover seems to be a trial of patience rather than truth. Both he who

has the strength to endure it conceals the truth, and so does he who has not. For why should pain sooner make me confess what is, than force me to say what is not?

For himself, Montaigne prefers 'to hold on to the solid and the probable', what lies closer to hand. 'Our life,' he says, 'is too real and essential to support these supernatural and fantastic accidents.' And sounding the bass note of compassion that underlines his work, he concludes: 'After all, it is putting a very high price on one's conjectures to have a man roasted alive for them.'

Montaigne thus sees human knowledge as needing to return to tangible objects: he describes touch as the sense that is 'nearer, more vivid and substantial' and able to 'overthrow all those fine stoical resolutions'. Moreover, it is a belief that characterizes not only the symphony of the 'Apology', but some of his earliest essays, such as 'Our Feelings Extend Beyond Ourselves', and 'How the Soul Discharges Her Passions Against False Objects Where the True Ones Are Wanting'. Here Montaigne finds 'the most universal of human errors' to be 'always gaping after future things':

> We are never at home, we are always beyond ourselves. Fear, desire, hope, still push us on toward the future, and deprive us of the feeling and consideration of that which is, to distract us with the thought of what will be, even when we shall be no more.

And yet we cannot escape our tactile, proximate awareness of human affairs. He tells how Edward I of England asked that after his death his bones should be carried in campaigns against the Scots, and he relates how an acquaintance of his would curse and rail at the sausages and hams which he saw as having caused his gout. He tells how men chew and swallow cards and choke themselves on the dice that they feel have cheated them. After seeing a bridge he had built destroyed, Xerxes of Persia attempted to have the Hellespont whipped and put in chains. And even in terms of our most abstract speculations:

> ... just as the arm when it is raised to strike, pains us if it misses the blow and meets only with the air ... The mind when it is agitated and in motion becomes lost within itself if it is not given something to take hold of ... just as animals attack the stone or the metal that has been thrown at them . . . what do we not choose to blame, rightly or wrongly, so as to have something at which to push.

Montaigne's sympathy for Sebond, and his impatience with his detractors, is based on his sense that all our knowledge – natural and theological alike – needs to be grounded in people, places, things – not least our own bodies and selves. And whilst this might be seen to align him conveniently with the rituals of Catholicism – he says that Protestants have tried to establish 'a purely contemplative and immaterial faith' that will merely slip through their fingers – it also strikes a chord with Montaigne's original impulse in writing: his attempt to rein in his flyaway mind – idly flickering like the reflections on water in a vat – by bringing it into contact with the task of writing, something that can be seen and heard and felt.

But here, Montaigne finds inspiration from not only

Sebond's theology, but his zoology, the circus of God's creation: for Sebond a text that could not be lost or deleted; for Montaigne, a squawking, squealing symphony that he found impossible to ignore.

6

When I Am Playing with My Cat, How Do I Know She Is Not Playing with Me?

As you wander through the Musée d'Aquitaine in Bordeaux – making your way to Montaigne's tomb, now situated near the way out – you come across an exhibit whose innocent freshness seems to provide a shelter against the ponderous weight of the past. A Gallo-Roman statue of a young girl, from around the second century CE, accompanied by a cockerel, and holding in front of her – as if posing for a picture – her cat. It's a simple enough image, but one that seems to skip across history somehow, as if all that divides you from the girl, with her cat, her bracelets, and her wide-open eyes, is little more than a thin pane of time.

And perhaps that was the intention of the man who commissioned it, inscribing it, 'Laetus . . . Father'. What he thought about her death we don't know. Perhaps he looked optimistically into her future, seeing her with her cat, and the cockerel for good measure, playing in a field of asphodels in the ever-morning of the afterlife. But her death signalled an alteration all the same, and to that, in the shape of this gravestone, he paid attention, in employing the sculptor to keep somehow some part of her near.

Montaigne seems less recognizable from his sarcophagus, lying short and fully armed on top of it, a bit like a tin soldier. But if he slips down from it on hot summer nights, and walks around the museum, you feel that this is a sculpture he would have liked. He also had a daughter. He liked animals too. And after resting for a while in its naturalism, he may have noticed a resemblance between the round-faced, wide-eyed little girl and her wide-eyed little cat, which the sculptor seems to see through his fingers. The father loved his daughter, and he was fond of the cat too: for in looking at the cat he looked at her.

❧

We have always noticed similarities between ourselves and other animals. We have cat-fights and bear-hugs, we feel bird-brained and sheepish. And if all goes to the dogs, we can resort to calling people pigs, chickens, or cows – or reach for that symbol of our over-eating, over-heated age: the beached whale. This may just be horsing around, but the more we look at history, the more our debts to animals emerge: where they stand as the silvering to the mirror of ourselves, a differential equation through which our humanness is constantly worked out.

For instance, the word 'cat' comes from the Latin *catus*, which could also mean quick-witted or cunning (the Egyptians rather charmingly called their cats *miew*). But deciding which came first, the cat or cat-like cunning, results in a sort of chicken-and-egg situation. The Chamber of the Bulls in the caves of Lascaux, sixty miles east of Montaigne, displays the antiquity of man's obsession with animals, yet in a cave whose echoing acoustics also suggest his wonder at the bullishness within himself (interestingly, in Lascaux's Chamber of Felines, with its seven prowling lions, the acoustics are much subtler).

And throughout human history the animal alphabet has provided a long-running index of human behaviour. Aesop in his fables saw animals as a rich source of moral insight, as did Aristophanes in *The Frogs* and *The Birds*. The Athenian Triptolemus concluded in his three laws that you should honour your parents, not hurt animals, and make offerings of fruit to the Gods instead. And in the bestiaries – animal encyclopedias – of the Middle Ages, we see a fascinating overlap between animals and humans: similarities that humans could never really escape from, living in such proximity to animals and being animals themselves.

To the medieval mind it was noted that in the Bible animals had been created before man, whom they were therefore intended to serve. This could be as food, or by working as beasts of the field, or simply to provide light entertainment, like peacocks and chimps. In the case of lions and bears, they were there to remind us of God's roar. But philosophers like Thomas Aquinas began to theorize about the differences between animals and ourselves and explained that animals lacked reason – specifically, the ability to look into the past or the future. Our humanness was therefore to some extent in inverse proportion to our animality: the further you moved away from animals the more human you were.

At the same time, animals and humans were often seen to share attributes. It could be said that the medieval mind looked for resemblances rather than differences when analysing phenomena, and animals served as convenient analogues of moral and spiritual virtues. A twelfth-century bestiary tells how a weasel's sniff-sniffing represents those who hear the word of God but are easily distracted. It describes how the male beaver, whose testicles were thought to have medicinal value, bites them off if being pursued and throws them in the hunter's face. If hunted for a second time, he displays his self-mutilation: 'For when the hunter sees that the beaver lacks testicles, he leaves him alone' – amazingly, this served as an allegory of how we should renounce our sins and throw them in the face of the devil, who will then stop molesting us. The twelfth-century philosopher Jacob ibn-Zaddik thus concluded: 'There is nothing in the world which has not its

correspondence in man . . . He is courageous like the lion, timorous like the hare, patient like the lamb, clever like the fox.'

But these resemblances could also work in both directions – from animal to human but also from human back again. In his *De humana physiognomonia* of 1586, Giambattista della Porta showed how a man's face was an augury of his destiny, linked to the animal he most resembled, such as a horse or a lion.

And in the literature of the sixteenth century animals were constantly invoked as defining the baser aspects of human behaviour. The scandal of Machiavelli's *The Prince* (1513), lay in his advice that a Prince ought intentionally to wallow in his animal nature: 'So, as a prince is forced to know how to act like a beast, he must learn from the fox and the lion; because the lion is defenceless against traps and a fox is defenceless against wolves.'

Montaigne's writing is filled with animals – the clucking, whinnying, scratching soundtrack of the *gentilhomme campagnard*. He talks knowledgeably about husbandry and hunting. He looks into his poultry yard and wonders how the cock knows when to crow. But pride of place in Montaigne's menagerie, and in keeping with his status as a seigneur, is, of course, the horse.

The short-statured Montaigne felt most at home in the saddle: 'I do not alight eagerly when I am on horseback; it is where I feel most at ease, whether healthy or sick.' He displays a nobleman's love of riding, and discusses the art of buying a horse, of examining the 'beauty of his colour or the breadth of his hindquarters . . . his legs, his eyes, and feet'. A badly fixed rein or a loose strap will put him in a bad mood all day. And in his account of the melancholy that followed his retirement, he likens his mind to 'a runaway horse' that his writing will attempt to break-in and subdue. He goes on to compare discourse to a horse, remarking that a horse's 'true strength is shown in making a sharp and sudden stop'. And pulls up his sentence there.

It could be said that early modern French had almost as many words for horses as the mythical fifty Inuit words for snow – *destrier*, *palefroi*, *haquenée*, *haridelle*, *pouter*, *poulin* and *roussin* – such were the variety of uses to which horses were put. The first meant a war-horse, to which Montaigne devotes an essay, the last meant a packhorse, the horse ridden by the servant who ploughed into Montaigne when he was out riding. But it was also Don Quixote's mount, from which after four days' deliberation he derived a name – 'Rocinante', meaning an ex-packhorse – obviously an analogy for the aged Don himself. And this fascination with the relationship between horse and rider posts untiringly through history: from Bucephalus to Black Bess and Black Beauty, whose adventures even Wittgenstein was reading when he died.

Montaigne is no exception. In his essay on war-horses he describes how Bucephalus looked like a bull (in this resembling Alexander himself), and would allow no one else to ride him. Grieving at his death, Alexander named a city in his honour (Bucephela, what is now Jhelum in Pakistan). Caesar's horse had forefeet like a man, the hooves divided like toes, which Caesar would ride bareback with no hands at full pelt, notes the admiring Montaigne.

He goes on to tell how the Islamic Mamelukes boasted the world's finest cavalry horses, that could tell friend from foe and would join in the battle kicking and biting, and could pick up lances and arrows with their teeth. The conquistadors, feeling rather well-heeled, went so far as to adorn their mounts with horseshoes made of gold. On the other hand, the army of Bajazet, frozen by the Russian winter, found a final use for their horses by disembowelling them and climbing inside. Montaigne pauses as if to allow his reader to take breath, then says: 'Let us carry on, since we are here.'

In an essay 'Of Riding Post', he tells how in Romania the couriers of the Grand Sultan travel at extraordinary speeds, having the right to demand a fresh horse from anyone they meet, and giving them their exhausted animals in return. But he sees the French as the best horsemen in the world – the reason, according to Tasso, why their legs are so short. He sees a man riding with both feet on the saddle, take the saddle off and put it on again, pluck something from off the ground and shoot backwards with a bow, all whilst riding at full gallop. On the other hand another Frenchman, the eccentric theologian Pierre Pol, rode round Paris side-saddle – 'like a woman', chuckles Montaigne.

He reserves a special disdain for coaches, which are effeminate and make him feel sick. He can't stand them, or litters, or boats, and 'all other riding but on horseback, both in town and country'. He cites the degeneracy of Heliogabalus 'the most effeminate man in the world', who had his coach drawn by two stags, and at other times by four naked women, 'having himself drawn by them in pomp totally nude'. The Emperor Firmus had his coach drawn by two ostriches of enormous size, so that it looked like he was taking to the air.

But as for Montaigne, horseback is the place to be. He would 'rather be a good horseman than a good logician' and would prefer to die on a horse than die in his bed. He notes how Plato prescribes riding for our general health, and Pliny says it is good for the stomach and the joints. For in riding,

the body is neither idle or exhausted, and the moderate agitation keeps it fit. Despite suffering with the stone, I can stay on horseback without dismounting or becoming weary, for eight or ten hours at a time . . .

For Montaigne 'being consists in movement' and he travels in the Spanish fashion, in long stages, rather than stopping for meals, saying that 'my horses are better for it'. He waters them as often as he can, taking care that they have enough time to absorb their water between stops, and claims that none has failed him that lasted the first day. Moreover, interesting thoughts strike him 'where I least expect them . . . on horseback, at table, and in bed; but mostly on horseback, where I am most given to thinking'.

And the thinking that emerges as Montaigne clops along is a new inquisitiveness about the capacities of animals, but one that stands in stark contrast to the general intellectual trajectory of the age.

∝

The humanist movement, in the spirit of which Montaigne had been trained, saw the essence of humanity in man's capacity for language, the thing that distinguished him from beasts. But the upward mobility that was characteristic of Renaissance humanism resulted in an increasing separation between ourselves and our four-legged friends. Human potential was on the up, but as a result the rest of creation received a dumbing-down. Thus, in one of the manifestos of humanism, Pico della Mirandola's *Oration on the Dignity of Man* (1486), he calls on animals to contradistinguish human ambition:

> 'Man is an animal of diverse, multiform and destructible nature.' But why do I emphasize this? In order for us to understand that, after having been born in this state so that we may be what we will to be, then, since we are held in honour, we ought to take particular care that no one

may say against us that we do not know that we are made similar to brutes and mindless beasts of burden.

The Dutch humanist Desiderus Erasmus, in his *Handbook of a Christian Soldier* (1503), says similarly that man is 'of a soul as of a certain goodly thing, and of a body as it were a brute or dumb beast'. But advises that through the scripture and the love of God one can move up the food chain:

> Embrace zealously this rule, not to be willing to crawl along the ground with unclean animals, but supported on those wings whose growth Plato thinks are induced in our minds by the heat of love and shoot out anew, raise yourself as on the steps of Jacob's ladder from the body to the spirit, from the visible to the invisible, from the letter to the mystery, from sensible things to intelligibile things . . .

Central to Erasmus's optimism is the translation from the 'letter' to the 'spirit' of the word of God – i.e. biblical literacy and understanding. And it was this humanistic, literate upturn, augmented by the increase in literacy following the invention of print, that led to language, rather than reason alone, being increasingly seen as the distinguishing mark of the human. With the proliferation of printed texts, language became more visible, making it obvious that animals didn't read. In the seventeenth century Edward Reynolds thus concluded that it was a clear symptom of 'melancholy' – i.e. madness – to think that 'Elephants and Birds, and other Creatures have a language whereby they discourse with one another.'

Others added to this sense of animals as increasingly tongue-tethered, and hence more contemptible than ourselves. Shakespeare's Hamlet reserves his basest terms of vituperation for his widowed mother, whom he sees as having lustfully, *animalistically*, taken Hamlet's uncle as her husband too soon: 'O God, a beast that wants discourse of reason / Would have mourned longer!'; and compares her to a pig: 'Stewed in corruption, honeying and making love / Over the nasty sty'. The dumb show that opens 'The Mousetrap', Hamlet's play-within-a-play designed to catch the conscience of Claudius, is thus not only a plot device, but a horrifying portrayal of his mother's 'dumb' bestial oblivion.

But it could also be said that things were not looking good for animals more generally. In the increasingly polarized world of Reformation Europe, animality became a common language of abuse. Protestants pictured the Pope as the 'Beast of the Apocalypse' and Luther published a pamphlet describing the allegorical appearance of a Pope-Ass and a Monk-Calf. People's lived experience of animals was also becoming more distant and penned-in. In the expanding towns of the sixteenth century, people had a less organic, mutually dependent relationship with animals, and experienced them more as parasites and pests – like dogs, or rats – or saw them simply as meat. And as markets expanded and liquidity increased, animals were increasingly traded and trafficked, slaughtered and skinned with little by way of sentiment.

The logical conclusion to this devaluing of animals came in Descartes' *Discourse on Method* (1637), with his theory of animals as 'beast-machines'. Aristotle had argued that animals possessed 'animals spirits' which gave them movement, something that they shared with human beings. But for Descartes animal movement could be understood simply as mechanical activity – an extension of the clockwork mechanism of the universe. Man's body could also be understood along mechanical lines, but the difference was that animals act *only* in accordance with the 'disposition of their organs' – like automata – and never 'use speech or other signs as we do when placing our thoughts on record for the benefit of others'.

It was thus not simply reason – the ability to look into the future and the past – but an inward, cognitive self-awareness that was seen to separate animals from ourselves: it was this that speech gave utterance to. The physician Walter Charlton, writing soon after Descartes, hence claimed:

> . . . nothing comes nearer to a manifest absurdity, than to suppose, that a Dogg can, as it were, say within himself, *I imagine that I do imagine*, or *I perceive that I am perceiving essence*, and the like; which is an action of such singular eminence above all what we observe to proceed from Doggs, or any of the most able and cunning Beasts in nature.

But the unpleasant upshot of this amongst some of Descartes' followers was that animals were therefore denied feeling. As Nicolas Malebranche cruelly concluded: 'They eat without pleasure, cry without pain, grow without knowing it; they desire nothing, fear nothing, know nothing' – and reportedly kicked a dog by way of illustration.

The human perfection that was heralded by the humanist project seemed to have been achieved: man had erected a barbed-wire fence of language and consciousness between himself and other animals. Not only were they inferior, but they were qualitatively different too. Man became the measure of all things – 'the lords and masters of nature', as Descartes put it – but animals were the necessary scapegoats. The Aristotelian reins that had tied us to our fellow creatures were let go.

But here Montaigne is remarkable for his intellectual independence. For Montaigne, it is not that animals do not possess language, but simply that we *do not understand them* –

> By a certain bark, the horse knows that a dog is angry, at another sound he is not afraid. Even in animals that have no voice, by the reciprocal kindnesses that we see between them, we can easily argue for another form of communication: their movements converse and discourse.

Here, in the central section of the 'Apology', using examples taken from Sextus and Plutarch, Montaigne allows his interest in animals to take centre-stage. In it he brackets human reason by looking at how other creatures possess knowledge of the world and conduct themselves in sympathy rather than in opposition to nature. He cites Aristotle on the way partridges give different calls, depending on their whereabouts. And whilst we don't understand animals, they understand us, and we unconsciously adjust the language we use to them without even knowing it:

> In what a variety different ways do we speak to our dogs, and they reply to us? With another language, and with other words, we summon birds, hogs, oxen, horses, and change the idiom according to is the species.

In a sense, therefore, Montaigne continues in the very essence of humanism – translating and extending our linguistic capacities – but keeps going, beyond Latin and Greek, into Dog, Horse, and Partridge, pushing at the very boundaries of linguistic exchange – 'rattling', as he says elsewhere, 'the last fences and barriers of knowledge'.

As a result, animals should never be patronized. Montaigne relates Plutarch's story about how a barber's magpie could imitate anything anyone said. Then one day some trumpeters stopped and blew a fanfare in front of the shop, after which the magpie was 'pensive, mute and melancholy' to the extent that everyone thought the sound had humbled her and made her dumb. All this time, however, she was studying the score in her head, as was seen when she broke forth 'expressing perfectly their melodies, pitches, and variations'. Elephants, Montaigne wonders, may have religion, as after many 'ablutions and purifications' we see them raising their trunks towards the rising sun and 'standing still a long time in meditation and contemplation'.

And some animals may be not only articulate, but numerate: the oxen at the palace of Susa in Persia had been trained to draw up water with a hundred turns a day, but in a bovine work-to-rule refused to work a minute's overturn. We are in our adolescence, Montaigne notes, before we can count this high. And even on the lowest level, creatures have negotiating skills that any Renaissance diplomat would admire. The philosopher Cleanthes patiently puzzled over a parley between two groups of ants, until a worm was paid in ransom and the body of the dead ant in question was chivalrously brought out.

Watching swallows, Montaigne admires their knowledge of raw materials, but also their gentleness in gathering moss for their nests so that 'the tender limbs of their young will lie there more softly and comfortably'. Is there a better ordered society than that of honey bees, asks Montaigne? Spiders know how to slacken and draw in their webs. He notes how animals go to war and tells of how the siege of Tamly was lifted after the besieging army was routed by bees. Moreover, 'upon their return from combat not a bee was missing'. Animals also know how to minister to themselves, notes the hypochondriac Montaigne. Tortoises purge themselves with marjoram. Storks dose themselves with sea-water enemas. Elephants pluck arrows and javelins from not only themselves but the limbs of their masters. To say that this is simply done from nature is to deny them 'science and wisdom'.

But the lesson for Montaigne is that our habitual species arrogance – that we think ourselves better than animals – could equally well be a symptom of our ignorance:

> The defect that prevents communication between them and us, why can't it be ours as much as theirs? It is still unknown whose fault it is that we don't understand each other – for we understand them no more than they do us. For by the same reason they may think us as brutish as we think them.

And with this, our assumed moral ascendancy over animals is put into question. According to Democritus, we have learned many of our abilities from animals: the spider to weave and sew, the swallow to build, the swan and the nightingale to sing (one genuinely wonders whether, if birds had not existed, man would have ever have imagined that he could fly). Fish in their iridescent beauty and symmetry are more attractive than ourselves. It is thus a result of the 'vanity' of his imagination that man:

> attributes divine qualities to himself, withdraws and separates himself from the mass of other creatures, distributes the shares of the animals, his fellows and companions, and allocates to them such portions of

faculties as he himself thinks fit. How does he know, by the efforts of his intelligence, the secret and internal motions of animals? From what comparison between them and us does he conclude the stupidity he attributes to them?

For in many ways, animals seem to be better adapted to life than ourselves, nature 'accompanying and leading them by the hand'. The Greek sceptic Pyrrho was stuck aboard a small boat during a storm, his fellow travellers terrified by the wind and the waves and the thought of death. But Pyrrho noticed a pig on board that was sitting out the tempest with porcine equanimity, pointing him out to his fellow men as an example to follow. 'What good is the knowledge of things,' asks Montaigne, 'if it puts us into a worse condition than Pyrrho's pig?'

And yet against the Cartesian charge that animals lack 'inner' sentience, Montaigne tells how, just as he is able conjure up an image of Paris by the power of his imagination,

> the same privilege, I say, seems clearly evident in animals: for a horse accustomed to trumpets, arquebuses, and warfare, we see twitching, and trembling in his sleep, as he lies on his straw, even as if he were in the midst of things. It is clear that he conceives in his mind the sound of a drum without noise, an army without arms or body . . . The hare that a greyhound imagines in a dream, after which we see him panting, stretching out his tail, twitching his thighs, and perfectly representing the movements of the chase: it is a hare without fur, without bones.

In their dreams, their hopes, their desires and unconscious fears, animals are no different from ourselves, if only we bothered to look. He relates an episode that occurred during the conquest of Mexico:

> When the Spaniards first arrived among the newly discovered people of the Indies, the Mexicans had such an opinion of them and their horses, that they saw them as gods and animals ennobled above their nature. Some, after they were conquered, and coming to ask for peace and forgiveness, bearing gold and provisions, did not fail to offer the same to the horses, with the same language they had used to the men, and interpreting their neighing for a language of conciliation and truce.

It is a complex moment of cultural and zoological translation. A less interested writer would view the actions of the Aztecs as stupidly mistaken, and make a joke. But Montaigne doesn't. What he notices is that, free of 'civilized' assumptions, the Aztecs saw something that the Spaniards hadn't – that their horses might be sophisticated creatures with the ability to communicate. But what is interesting is the way Montaigne leaves the Spaniards out of the discussion, in which a truce of friendship and trust is sealed, not between themselves and the Aztecs, but between the Aztecs and the horses. In a moment of conquest the Spaniards are kept in the dark, and in triumph are outwitted, without even knowing it.

Animals thus offer a chastening reminder of our place in creation, and Montaigne recognizes 'a certain commerce, between them and us, and a certain mutual obligation': 'We live, both them and us, under the same roof and inhale the same air: there is, save for more or less, a perpetual resemblance between us.' He thus confesses to a nature so childishly tender that he 'cannot easily refuse my dog when he offers to play with me, even at an inopportune moment'. Moreover, humanity has a 'duty' not only to animals but also 'to trees and plants'; he notes how the immoderation of our appetite has outstripped 'all the inventions by which we attempt to satisfy it'. All this he says in order 'to bring us back and join in the great mass of creation' and see 'the resemblance there is in all living things'.

But what is equally important for Montaigne is what animals reveal about ourselves. And here they serve not simply as a check on our presumption, but as a guide to the trail that leads out of our sceptical enclosure: that there might be another answer to the question – *Que sçais-je?* – but one to which we have almost become blind.

For as Montaigne annotated his final edition of the *Essays* in the years before his death, he added to his disquisition on animals a livelier image, but one that perhaps helps to sum up his attitude as a whole:

> When I am playing with my cat, how do I know
> she is not playing with me?

The phrase has become famous as an expression of Montaignean scepticism – i.e. we don't know whether pets are playing with us or not; we are too ignorant to ever really know (and here one might emphasize the literal sense of the original French: 'qui sçait si elle passe son temps de moy plus que je ne fay d'elle?' / 'who knows if she passes her time more with me than I do with her?'). That is to say, rather than her being *his* pet, is he *hers*? (Or, as the seventeenth-century writer Samuel Butler cynically quipped: 'As Montaigne, playing with his cat, / Complains she thought him but an ass . . .')

But Montaigne then goes on to make another addition to his essay, one that survives in the posthumously published 1595 edition:

> We ourselves entertain with similar apish tricks. If I have my hour to begin or refuse, also she has hers.

And here it is clear that Montaigne is saying that he *does* know she is playing with him, as he is able to see his own experience (of wanting or refusing to play) reflected in her actions. Once he overcomes his 'natural presumption' of species superiority, he is able to read and understand her movements and gestures, as she can his. And significant here is the shift from the 'I' and the 'she' to the reflexive 'we' ('Nous nous entretenons . . .'). From a position of separation and distance, of two separate identities, two different species, Montaigne and his cat become, in their mutual playfulness, one. Not exactly one soul in two bodies, but two bodies sharing the same movements, gestures, and thoughts.

But the important point is that this reciprocal awareness is achieved not despite their lack of linguistic exchange, but *because of it*: it is a proximate language of touch and gesture, of caresses and playful taps that brings about a mutual understanding. And in his additions to the Bordeaux edition he goes on to expand:

> Plato, in his picture of the golden age under Saturn, considered among the principal advantages of man during that time was his communication with animals; by inquiring and receiving instruction from them, he knew the true qualities and differences of each of them, acquiring as a result a greater understanding and wisdom and conducting his life far more happily than we are able to do now.

Animals, themselves in touch with the 'necessary, tangible and palpable' benefits of nature, can thus serve to instruct man. And whilst we think we cannot communicate with them, the truth is that we once could, and in fact still can: 'They fawn on us, threaten us, demand of us, and we them.' He tells how horses form 'a certain acquaintance with one another' and greet each other 'with joy and demonstrations of goodwill'. Moreover, this free and frank communication is shared not only within 'the same species, but also of different species'. He goes on to note examples of affection flourishing between animals and humans, such as Plutarch's reluctance to sell an old and faithful ox; or the elephant who courted an Alexandrian flower-girl with fruit before slipping his trunk into her blouse in order to 'tastoit les tettins', as Montaigne puts it.

But what is most important for Montaigne is how this recognition of animal communication is a springboard to a new conception of the human: how despite their sectarian divisions – where there seems to be 'more difference between one man and another than between some animals and some men' – this divisiveness might be able to be overcome. And what is also significant is that it is a restoration that flies in the face of Montaigne's entire humanist education. He therefore observes how deaf mutes:

> dispute, argue, and tell stories by signs. I have seen some so supple and practised in it that in truth they were not short of perfection in their ability to make themselves understood. Lovers grow angry, become reconciled, beg, give thanks, make assignations, and in short, say everything with their eyes.

He quotes Torquato Tasso on the capacity of silence itself to entreat and talk, and speculates that speech is not necessarily natural or essential. And then, in a lengthy comment added to his final edition, Montaigne completes the circle from animal-to-human to human-to-human again, concluding that we cannot help but communicate ourselves in some way, that *our own* movements *'converse and discourse'* – even if it is something to which we are habitually blind:

> What of the hands? We request, we promise, call, dismiss, menace, pray, supplicate, deny, refuse, interrogate, admire, count, confess, repent, fear, are ashamed, doubt, instruct, command, incite, encourage, swear, testify, accuse, condemn, absolve, insult, despise, challenge, taunt, flatter, applaud, bless, humiliate, mock, reconcile, recommend, exalt, congratulate, rejoice, complain, grieve, despair, depress, are astonished, exclaim, keep quiet – and with a manifold variation that is the envy of the tongue. With the head we invite, dismiss, avow, disavow, contradict, welcome, honour, revere, disdain, demand, spurn, enliven, lament, caress, rebuke, submit, defy, exhort, menace, assure, inquire. What of the eyebrows? What of the shoulders? There is not a movement that does not speak, and in a language intelligible without instruction, a language that is common to all. From which it follows, seeing the variety and differences between other languages, that this one ought to be judged the true language of human nature.

The true language of human nature – of course we would be wrong to take it as a serious proposition that we should use gestures instead of words. But what is interesting about Montaigne's list is that it incorporates friendship but also enmity: we flatter, honour and welcome, but also menace, rebuke and defy. Even when we think we are severing human relations we are forging them. And this opens the way to a cautious optimism: that despite the rifts and divisions opened up by civil war, people retain the ability to communicate with each other. Our bodies are engaged in a form of commerce that ties us together, despite the differences in our thoughts – as Montaigne, inspired by the example of animals observes:

> There are certain inclinations of affection that are sometimes born in us without the advice of reason, coming from an accident of fortune which others call sympathy; of this animals are as capable as ourselves.

Despite our political and religious differences, men have an inbuilt disposition towards communication, and the recognition of this will allow truth – or rather trust – to find a way through.

Montaigne's fascination with animals is, of course, built up out of a piebald congregation of fact and half-fact, anecdote, fable and shaggy-dog tales. And although we cannot really learn anything in detail about animals from Montaigne, about their real behaviour, or whether they are or are not 'conscious' (although whether such issues should be seen as the basis of our actions towards them is a moot point), what we can learn is that it is sometimes useful to let our minds off the leash for a moment. Unlike Descartes and many later thinkers, Montaigne doesn't erect a fence between ourselves and animals, but sees human beings as part of the greater chain of creation – what we would now call evolution – a fact that makes him more humane than many writers before or since.

And perhaps this belief that animals can tell us something about ourselves, even in terms of what we lack, was maybe Wittgenstein's motive in reading *Black Beauty* as he lay dying of throat cancer in Cambridge in 1951. Wittgenstein had a keen interest in the worldview of other creatures. His *Philosophical Investigations* features a duck-rabbit, a goose, a cow, a lion and a hypocritical dog. Whilst staying in a remote cottage in Connemara on the west coast of Ireland, he would tame robins and chaffinches to eat from his hand. It was said that he classified his Cambridge colleagues in terms of the animals they most resembled. He may also, it has been claimed, have suffered from Asperger's syndrome – manifested in his craving for order and predictability and a difficulty in dealing with the complexity of normal human affairs.

Hence, perhaps, his interest in *Black Beauty: The Autobiography of a Horse*, written by the invalided Anna Sewell in 1877 to educate people in the suffering experienced by horses. Sewell's brave innovation was to narrate the story purely from the horse's point of view, announcing on the title page: 'translated from the equine'. We thus hear of Beauty's working life and his dealings with his sometimes kind, but often cruel, human owners. But at the end of the book he is put out to pasture, and here, on the last page, finally recovers his natural equanimity:

Willie always speaks to me when he can, and treats me as his special friend. My ladies have promised that I shall never be sold, and so I have nothing to fear; and here my story ends. My troubles are all over, and I am at home; and often before I am quite awake, I fancy I am still in the orchard at Birtwick, standing with my old friends under the apple-trees.

Wittgenstein had spent much of his life philosophizing about how one might give up philosophy. Here, as he lay at the end of his brilliant but somewhat lonely life, might he have glimpsed such a vision in Beauty's last days: a moment of tranquillity, with friends near to hand, untroubled by the squalls and hurricanes of philosophical doubt: finally, philosophically, 'at home'?

For Montaigne, like Wittgenstein, animals are interesting because they help us to think about such things. For Montaigne, his cat similarly allows him think about stepping outside himself, to think about what it is to be her, and therefore to think what it is to be himself. And here, although there are no firm conclusions, he seems to imply that we can learn as much from comparing as we can by contrasting ourselves to other creatures – as Charles Darwin was to do three centuries later in his *Expression of the Emotions in Man and Animals* of 1872.

But here we are back with *catus*: the cat-like cunning that the Romans recognized in what is now for us simply a noun. Did this linguistic overlap between animal and human result from an intellectual simplicity but also a maturity, as manifested in their belief in satyrs and centaurs and fauns? And was this perhaps the reason for Laetus' inclusion of the cat on his daughter's gravestone: to give a more meaningful account of her essence, an essence that wasn't an essence, but a babbling menagerie of her gestures and actions – an unfinished symphony of animal, human, female, feline, playful, cockerel, *catus*?

We will never know. The cat maintains its marble-eyed constancy. But perhaps, as Montaigne says, there is sometimes wisdom in not speaking, a thing that we do well to remember. He tells how the ambassador of Abdera spoke to King Agis of Sparta at great length, then asked what answer he should take back to his citizens. The King replied: 'That I let you say whatever you wanted, for as long as you wanted, without even saying a word.'

'Wasn't that an intelligent and eloquent silence?' remarks Montaigne.

7

To Rub and Polish Our Brains with Others

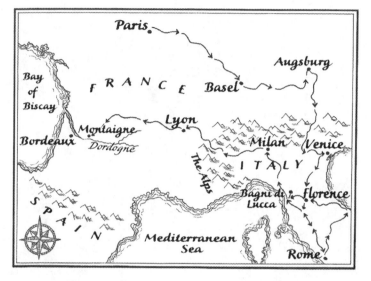

Route of Montaigne's trip to Italy, 1580–81

With the 'Apology for Raymond Sebond' as its intellectual centrepiece, Montaigne put the finishing touches to what would be the first edition of his work, bought paper laid with a heart-shaped watermark, and took his manuscript downstream to the printing house of Simon Millanges in Bordeaux. He was forty-seven, and recorded the date as 1 March 1580, at the end of the address 'To the Reader' that he placed at the front of his book:

> You have here a book of good faith, reader. It tells you at the outset that I have here proposed to myself no other aim but a domestic and private one. I have here had no consideration for your service or my glory. My powers are not capable of such a design. I have dedicated it to the particular commodity of my family and friends, so that when they have lost me (which they must do soon), they will here retrieve some traits of my conditions and humours, and by that nourish entirely and vividly the knowledge they had of me. Had my intention been to seek the world's favour, I should have adorned myself with borrowed beauties, or have strained to draw myself up into my best posture. I want to be seen here in my simple, natural, and ordinary manner, without exertion or artifice: for it is myself I paint. My defects are there to be read to the life, and my natural form, so far as public decency permits me. If I had been placed among those nations which they say still live under the sweet liberty of the laws of nature, I assure you I would have most willingly have painted myself entirely and fully naked.

The final months had been a terrible scramble to get the text ready, with the pirated publication of La Boétie's *On Voluntary Servitude* ruining his plans to include it in his text, and the loss of an essay to a pilfering lackey. Montaigne needed a break.

And so a couple of months later, on 22 June, Montaigne loaded up horses and cart with food and clothing, copies of the *Essays* and barrels of wine, and set off on a seventeen-month trip through Switzerland, Germany, Austria, and Italy to Rome. Rome was the spiritual heartland of the Renaissance, yet his secretary writes that Montaigne would just as easily have gone off the beaten track – to Poland, Greece or someplace else. However, the opinions of his travelling companions prevailed; these were his youngest brother Bertrand de Mattecoulon, his brother-in-law Bernard de Cazalis, young Charles d'Estissac and a Monsieur du Hautoy, as well as a number of servants. Nonetheless, they often criticized Montaigne for leading them astray, to which he would testily reply that he 'was not going anywhere except where he found himself, and that he could not lose or go off his way, since he had no plan but to travel in unknown places'.

Our knowledge of the trip comes from the *Travel Journal* that Montaigne wrote on the way, a large part of which he dictated to a secretary, who transcribed it in the third person, the remainder of which he penned himself, writing in Italian in Italy and in French when returning home. Later he used his *Travel Journal* to augment the subsequent editions of the *Essays* – adding details about the bathhouses of Italy, the cruelty of public executions, and the madness of the Italian poet Torquato Tasso, whom he visited in Ferrara. But for the next two hundred years the manuscript was lost. It was eventually found by a local historian in a trunk at the château and published in 1774, only for its pages to be then scattered in the whirlwind of the French Revolution. Our knowledge of the *Travel Journal* thus goes back to this eighteenth-century edition, which records the missing first two pages of the manuscript in an opening worthy of Gabriel García Márquez:

> . . . Monsieur de Montaigne dispatched Monsieur de Mattecoulon post-haste with the said groom to visit the said Count, and found that his wounds were not fatal.

We therefore never discover the identity of the Count visited by Montaigne's brother, the nature of his injuries, nor, more generally, Montaigne's reasons for setting off in the first place.

The most likely explanations are to do with getting away from France and its religious wars and his sense of frustration at the responsibilities of household management. He may also have been feeling flush as a result of the growth of his estate. But he had other more personal reasons, too. Since the spring of 1578 Montaigne had been suffering increasingly from kidneys stones, and at the end of his first edition of the *Essays* we learn how he had tried the mineral baths of Chaudes-Aigues and Bagnères as a possible cure. The *Travel Journal* shows his desire to pursue the same cure in the mineral baths of Italy, especially the famous baths at Bagni di Lucca. Montaigne's journey thus becomes a voyage round his own body, as he plots the path of kidney stones through it, the movement of food and water into and out of it, to such an extent that nineteenth-century editors were so offended that they cut the riper sections out.

The other reason for Montaigne's trip was simply to travel: 'My object is only to keep in motion so long as the motion pleases me.' Travelling at the time was seen as a necessary evil, an uncomfortable and often dangerous activity. But Montaigne sees the benefits as outweighing the irritations – 'travelling does me no injury except in regard to the expense'. He had not seen the world through military service as had his father (who had also written his own journal of his travels to Italy). And there is a sense of him attempting to recapture his lost youth: at the time of setting off he was forty-seven and his companions were all at least twenty years younger. Travel thus became a way of restoring his own vitality:

> Travel is in my opinion a profitable exercise. The soul is there continually exercised in noticing new and unknown things, and I do not know a better school . . . in which to model life than by constantly suggesting to it the diversity of so many other lives, fancies and customs, and by allowing it to taste the perpetual variety of forms of our nature.

His secretary writes of the 'pleasure he took in visiting strange countries' which made him forget 'the weakness of his health and his age'. By travelling, Montaigne declares, one can 'rub and polish one's brain' through contact with others. And he displays an almost anthropological awareness of the body language and customs of other cultures – as well as a backpacker's obsession with them not ripping him off.

In the first section of his journey, Montaigne travels from his home to Paris, stopping off to present Henry III with a copy of the *Essays*. He then goes on to witness the siege of the Protestant-held La Fère, seventy miles to the north, before setting off along the banks of the Marne, down through eastern France and into Switzerland and Germany.

As Montaigne gets into his stride what emerges is his sense of the contrasts to his own country. In Germany he describes the variations in the time-keeping in the towns he visits – how in Germany the clocks strike the quarter hours, even the minutes (in Italy, clocks were much more uncommon, much to his chagrin). He records the price of horses, the size of loaves, the shape of hats, the types of wood available and how the villagers of Remiremont pay their yearly rent in snow. And if he doesn't understand, he asks. At the entrance to Lindau he notices an old wall, lacking any inscription, and upon asking around finds that its name in German means simply 'Old Wall'.

But what is also interesting is Montaigne's taste for the extraordinary, an intellectual disposition which is characteristic of the pre-scientific belief that Nature is understood not through the assembling of commonplaces but through the surprises that it has in store. He notes the echoes of the horses' hooves as he rides through the mountains, surrounding the traveller with a constant drumming. And at the baths of Plombières he meets the seigneur of d'Andelot, whose mourning for his brother had left a physical mark:

> Some of his beard was totally white, and a part of one eyebrow; and he told Monsieur de Montaigne that the change had come upon him in an instant, one day that he was at home full of grief at the death of one of his brothers, whom the Duke of Alva had put to death . . . his head was resting on his hand in that place and in such a way that those who were present thought it was some flour which had somehow fallen on it. It has remained so ever since.

He meets a Cremona merchant with dementia who cannot finish his Paternoster – 'never aware at the end that he had started, nor at the beginning that he had come to the end' – and who, somehow appropriately, wears a wide feather-brimmed hat. He visits the stables of the Duke of Florence, where he sees a strange sheep, a camel, and something 'the size of a very large mastiff in the shape of a cat, all patterned in black and white, which they call a tiger'.

Montaigne also exhibits an eager practical and technological interest, the mindset that was to become properly assembled in the scientific revolution. He learns from a carpenter how the number of rings on a tree are equal to its age, and sees the lathe and woodworking tools of the Duke of Poggio ('a very great mechanic' in his spare time). He visits a silver mine, a playing card factory and describes the workings of a water pump, a siphon, and a clockwork spit. He is called upon by Doctor Burro, of the University of Rome, who presents him with his book on the ebb and flow of the sea.

Some of his greatest wonderment is reserved for plumbing. In the ornamental gardens of Pratolino, he records how spouts drench the unwary tourist and water seeps from a marble washerwoman's laundry. At the Villa di Castello in Florence he sees a statue of the Apennines in the shape of an old man, 'from whose beard, forehead and hair water is constantly flowing, drop by drop, in order to represent sweat and tears'. He is tickled by the hydraulic horseplay of the gardens of the Fuggers in Augsburg, where 'thin, hard jets of water, to the height of man's head, fill the petticoats and thighs of the ladies with this coolness', taking them by surprise.

And he relaxes. He laughs at some comedians. He sends some actresses some fish. He enters a raffle (comes second), and rates the beauty of the famous prostitutes of Florence ('nothing special'). He goes shopping for souvenirs, buying a hooped silver barrel, an Indian cane, a vase and some Indian nut (good for the spleen). He visits the Vatican library and inspects Aristotle's untidy handwriting. He goes sledging down Mont Cenis: 'a pleasant bit of sport, without much risk'.

The quality of the hotels also provides a diversion: the Post at Piacenza is the best, the Falcon at Pavia the worst, and the Bear in Rome is very good (it still survives as an expensive restaurant). Here he was well treated, 'with three fine bedrooms, a dining-room, a larder, stable, kitchen, for twenty crowns a month, for which the landlord provided a cook and fire for the kitchen'.

And throughout, Montaigne remains constantly mindful of his nobility. He presents his favourite lodgings with a plaque bearing his coat of arms (azure powdered with trefoils). At Sterzing he dismisses the local schoolmaster as nothing but 'a fool'. In Rome he is so eager to salute another gentleman that he pokes himself in the eye (although from this incident he manages to salvage a joke, about the right thumb becoming left (*sinistre* = left/evil). But he can be deliberately vague about his status, in order that he might be mistaken for a baron or a knight, the equivalent of being upgraded to first class. Yet faced with an impertinent Italian coach-driver he returns to form, delivering him a box around the ears, thus proving the old saw that a true gentleman never hesitates before acting ungentlemanly.

But what makes Montaigne one of the most interesting travellers of the age is his genuine interest in the historical forces that were sweeping across Europe. As he enters Germany he moves into foreign territory, not only politically, but religiously, as the homeland of the Reformation. Here Montaigne attempts to put his own beliefs on hold and inquire about the progress of reform on the ground. At Isny, he goes and seeks out the local minister, and gets into a theological discussion over dinner. Here he plays devil's advocate, relaying the Calvinist criticism that Luther's teaching implies that God is not only in the host, but everywhere. At this things get a little heated, and 'this doctor denied with loud words this imputation, and defended himself from it as from a calumny' – (something that he did not do 'very well', Montaigne snorts to his journal). But at least he has the decency to escort Montaigne and d'Estissac to mass at a local monastery, where he stands aside and watches them at their prayers, albeit with his hat firmly on his head.

In Augsburg, perhaps the finest town in Germany, Montaigne sees Protestantism on the make. He visits a new Lutheran church which looks like a great college hall, bare of images, organs or crosses, the walls instead covered with verses from the Bible. And he notes the congregation is two or three times the size of the Catholic one. In Kempen he asks the minister whether dancing is allowed ('Of course'), and why the newly constructed organ has images of Christ painted on it when the old images on the church had been erased. This the minister blames on the Zwinglians' iconoclastic zeal, having no objection to images himself, provided they are not mistaken for the real thing. Warming to this inquisitive French nobleman, the minister, a Johannes Tilianus from Augsburg, invites him to his home and shows him his library – 'a handsome one, and well kitted-out'.

Elsewhere, pockets of the old Catholic superstition remain. At the Church of the Holy Cross in Augsburg Montaigne sees displayed a host that had turned into flesh, describing it as a little morsel 'with the redness of skin'. In Seefeld, the town is still in awe of the man who was swallowed up to his neck by the ground after greedily asking for a piece of the priest's larger Eucharist. You could still see the hole into which he plummeted, now covered with a grating, and the impression on the altar where he had desperately clung on.

Yet the Counter-Reformation's attempt to reform these superstitions is also under way. In Landsberg he goes to see the Jesuits, who are busy building a fine new church. If anyone here even dreams of any religion other than the Catholic, remarks Montaigne, 'he had better keep it quiet'. In Augsburg he also visits the Jesuits, finding some 'very learned'. But reform is rarely straightforward. In Icking the Jesuits have caused a commotion by forcing the priests to give up their concubines, who now complain so bitterly to the Duke that you would think what was merely tolerated 'was practised as if it was legitimate'.

But in traversing these religious boundaries Montaigne is quick to see the ironies and inconsistencies of religious zeal. The irascible Lutheran at Isny says brazenly over supper that he would 'rather hear a hundred masses than participate in the Calvinist communion'. In Italy, particularly in Rome, many of the churches have few images, and some old churches none at all. Moreover, raw from the French civil wars, Montaigne records optimistically the places where the two faiths peacefully cohabit. In Augsburg marriages of Lutherans and Catholics are common, 'the keener party submitting to the rules of the other'. Indeed the landlord of his inn, The Linden-Tree, is

Catholic and his wife Lutheran. And a good ecumenical team they make too, with their godly-clean house with its washed staircase covered in linen, and no sign of cobwebs or dirt.

South of Augsburg there is no more talk of Protestantism, and the Italian language starts about two leagues (about six miles) along the road to Trent. But as he passes into Italy, a slightly disapproving tone enters Montaigne's journal. He visits the Jesuates of St Jerome, a sort of religious order, the majority of whom he describes as 'ignorant', dressed in brown robes and little white hats, who spend their time distilling an orange liqueur. In Verona the men chat during mass with their hats on, only pausing during the elevation of the host. And again in Rome it 'seems strange' to Montaigne to see the Pope and his cardinals gossiping during the service. On Maundy Thursday he watches the Pope standing on the steps of St Peter's excommunicating 'an infinite number of people', including 'the Huguenots by that very name', and any princes who had seized Church lands – at the mention of whose names the cardinals de Medici and Caraffa 'laughed very heartily'. And in St Giovanni he again observes the slightly relaxed conduct of Catholicism as the Cardinal of San Sisto, sitting in the place usually taken by a penitent, taps the congregation on the head with a long wand as they pass, but courteously and smilingly so, and all the more 'according to their status and beauty'.

In Pisa theological standards plummet to a new low when the priests of the Cathedral and the friars of St Francesco get into a fight. It starts with an argument about who should conduct the funeral of a wealthy parishioner, but like a rookie reporter Montaigne gets down there as fast as he can, and constructs a blow-by-blow account:

A priest, approaching the high altar, tried to take hold

of the marble table. A friar attempted to drag him away. To whom the vicar, patron of this church of priests, gave a slap. Little by little, one thing led to another, and they came to fisticuffs, using sticks, candlesticks, torches and suchlike – they used everything.

Needless to say, the rich man's funeral mass went unsaid.

But Montaigne also witnesses a more sinister side to theological power. During Holy Week in Rome a priest displays the shroud, the cloth bearing Christ's image used by St Veronica to wipe his face: 'a repulsive face', Montaigne observes, 'in dark and sombre colours'. On seeing it the crowd become ecstatic, one woman stretched out, raving and screaming, 'said to be possessed'. And when Montaigne comes across an exorcist treating another demoniac – a melancholic, 'who seemed half dead' – a sinister religious puppetry seems to be at work:

They were holding him on his knees in front of the altar, with some kind of cloth around his neck by which they held him tight. The priest read from his breviary a number of prayers and exorcisms in his presence, commanding the Devil to leave his body. After this he directed his remarks to the patient, now speaking to him, now to the Devil in person, and then abusing him, hitting him hard with his fist, and spitting in his face. The patient responded to his demands with a few inept replies: now for himself, saying how he felt the stirrings of his affliction; now for the Devil, saying how he feared God, and how these exorcisms were effective against him.

After taking the pyx, the container in which the Eucharist is carried, and burning some candles by turning them upside down, the priest's imprecations reach a crescendo. He then unties the man and gives him back to his people to take home. He explains to the assembled spectators that this was one of the worst sort of obstinate devils, who took a great deal of work to cast out. Only the day before he had exorcized a woman, who had spat out nails, pins and tufts of hair. But when someone objects that she has still not recovered, he replies that she was now possessed by a lighter devil, 'for he knew their names, their divisions and particular distinctions'. Noting the absence of nails and hair in the present case, Montaigne's final observation seems sceptical, and perhaps, as a fellow lawyer (and fellow human being), his possessive 'my' shows he was touched with compassion:

> My man made no sign except to grind his teeth and twist his mouth when they presented the *Corpus Domini* to him, and occasionally mouthed these words: *Si fata volent* [If the fates will]; for he was a notary, and knew a little Latin.

Such moments are useful in balancing our view of Montaigne, who in the *Essays* professes an ostensibly conservative Catholicism, but who in his *Travel Journal* – a book not intended for publication – displays a more complex response: a questioning, slightly dissatisfied attitude towards the Church, even if, in the end, he is prepared to give it the benefit of the doubt.

For Montaigne still finds much to admire in Catholicism. The assembled devotion of the people moves him, especially in Holy Week when at night 'the whole city seemed to be in flames . . . every man bearing a torch, and almost always of white wax'. And he witnesses how the Pope's absolute power also encompasses forgiveness. On Palm Sunday he finds a boy sitting by the altar of the church, dressed in blue taffeta with a crown of olive branches and a lighted torch: 'He was a boy of fifteen or thereabouts, who, by the Pope's order had that day been liberated from prison. He had killed another boy.'

But in terms of the grandeur of Rome, the *terminus ad quem* of many Renaissance travellers, Montaigne seems equivocal. The humanistic impulse to travel saw the goal of the Grand Tour in terms of an exposure to classical civilization: where all roads – cultural, intellectual and moral – led to Rome, and with it a universal model of human perfection. But in his journal, Montaigne strikes a sceptical note, emphasizing the distance and irretrievability of antiquity, seeing it as a Renaissance or rebirth that will never reach full term, in a peroration that his secretary scrambles to take down:

> He said 'that one saw nothing of Rome but the sky under which it had been founded and the outline of its form; that the knowledge he had of it was abstract and contemplative, and founded on nothing perceptible to the senses . . . It often happened that after digging a long way down into the ground, they would only find the head of a very high column, which was still standing on its feet down below . . . It is easy to see that many streets are more than thirty feet below those of the present day.'

It is a speech that might be said to represent the end of the Renaissance and the beginning of modernity: where scepticism dislodges humanism from the driving seat of intellectual life.

But in its place Montaigne also ushers in a new sense of the importance of travel, one that places less emphasis on history and antiquity and more on the here-and-now. In his essay 'Of the Education of Children' Montaigne thus explores the idea that life is an education in itself, of which travel provides one of the most important lessons:

> but not in the fashion of our French nobles, simply to report on the length of Pantheon, or the sumptuousness of Signora Livia's drawers, or, like some others, how much longer or fatter the face of Nero is on some old ruin rather than on some medal; but to report mainly on the humours and manners of those nations, and to rub and polish our brains with others.

And in his 1580 edition of the *Essays* he emphasizes the sociable nature of travel: 'the pleasure of visiting many kinsmen and friends whom I have on the way, of the society which resorts there'. And this is borne out in the *Travel Journal*, where he displays a more ethnological outlook, an interest in the rituals and habits, movements and gestures of everyday life. And here, despite Montaigne's effort to fit in, speaking and writing in Italian when in Italy, his foreignness also bestows a certain privilege: silencing the distracting chatter of language, and allowing him to observe the grammar of human behaviour close at hand.

In Tuscany and Urbino he notes how the women curtsey in the French fashion, bending at the knees. In Baden you salute the ladies by kissing your hand and offering to touch their hand. They will simply stand still, as is their custom, or if you are lucky, slightly incline their head. In Germany, out of deference, you pass to the left of a man, leaving him free to put his hand to his weapon. And in Kempen Montaigne witnesses a modest wedding, but does not say so at first, leaving the simple actions and movements of the parties to speak for themselves:

> After the sermon the other minister went and placed himself at the altar with his face turned towards the people, having a book in his hand; a young woman presented herself to him, her head bare and her hair loose, who made a little curtsey, in the fashion of the country, and stood there alone. Soon a young man, who was an artisan, with a sword at his side, also came up and placed himself by the side of the woman. The minister said some words into their ear, and then told each of them to say the Paternoster, and then began to read out of a book. They were certain rules for those getting married; and he made them touch hands, one to the other, without kissing.

Even the most ancient rituals, he notes, are moulded by local customs, some receiving the Eucharist into their mouths and others reaching out to take it in their hands.

The poor also have their own conventions and customs. In Florence he is struck by the forwardness of the beggars, not only for their aggressiveness, but their hauteur: 'Give me alms, won't you!', or 'Give me something, do you hear!'; a Roman beggar similarly accosts Montaigne's conscience: 'Do good, for your own sake!' (It is whilst giving out money that Montaigne loses his wallet, dropping it through the vents in his breeches.) In Bagni di Lucca the locals display their local affiliation to the local French and Spanish factions by wearing flowers. In an attempt to fit in, Montaigne puts a flower in his left ear only to upset the French coterie as a result.

And in terms of Montaigne's tactile, sensory awareness,

things just *feel* different abroad. At the Dove in Markdorf, they fill their mattresses with leaves, finding it lasts better than straw. Montaigne tries sleeping with a feather quilt 'as is their custom' and finds it very pleasant, 'both warm and light'. He likes the stoves that they use in southern Germany, in not scorching one's face or boots, and being free from the smoke produced by fireplaces (which tend to offend Montaigne's sensitive nose).

And cultural differences are most clearly tasted in food, not only in what is eaten, but in terms of table manners and etiquette. In Lindau they chop up cabbage with a special implement to make sauerkraut, which they put in salted tubs for the winter. They mix up plum and pear and apple tarts with the meat course and sometimes serve the roast before the soup. This he eats in the dining room of the Crown, listening to the birds in a cage that stretches the whole length of the room. In Icking he drinks from wooden goblets ribbed and ringed like barrels; in Kempen he dines on white hare. At Innsbruck the preparations are so elaborate that the diners sit a little distance from the table, which is then lifted up and carried to them. He immerses himself in these differences without complaint, but his personal tastes strike one as rather modern for a seigneur. He likes fresh fruit, oranges, lemons and particularly melons. And he has a cultivated taste for the lightness of Italian cuisine. At Pontremoli he has 'olives without stones, dressed with oil and vinegar, like in a salad' – 'very good'.

This is not to say that Montaigne is incapable of prejudice. He cites the landlord of the Eagle in Constance as 'an example of the barbaric insolence and arrogance of the Teutonic character, over the quarrel of one of our footmen with our guide from Basel'. Appropriately, the quarrel is settled when the local provost, an Italian, displays a different national trait: he decides in Montaigne's favour if he dismisses his men, whilst allowing that he can immediately take them back into his service. 'This was a remarkable piece of subtlety,' admires Montaigne.

And Montaigne, like most of us, cannot help using what he knows to gauge the unknown. He sees life in Germany as more expensive than at home, and French walnut as superior to their pine. And he had heard rumours about how the Alps were 'full of difficulties, the strange manners of the people, the roads inaccessible, the inns savage'. Yet a little way into his trip, at Bressanone, he stops to reflect on the reality that travelling abroad is not necessarily more hazardous than travelling at home. The climate was mild, they had only had about one hour's rain, and 'in every other respect, if he wished to take his daughter, a girl only eight years old, on a journey, he would just as soon take her on this road as along one of the walks in his garden'. Moreover, Montaigne throws himself into the experience of difference, in stark contrast to the attitude of his companions who most of the time 'only wanted to go home'. He gets up 'with eagerness and alacrity' at the prospect of a new destination. He is constantly 'on the lookout for what he might encounter, and seeks every occasion for conversing with strangers'. He is annoyed in Rome to come across so many Frenchmen, and goes out of his way to melt into the background. He 'lets himself be served everywhere in the manner of each country'. In Augsburg he dresses plainly, puts on a fur hat in the manner of the locals and walks around town incognito. He is therefore somewhat distressed to find that he has blown his cover by blowing his nose (handkerchiefs were somewhat of a novelty at the time).

But Montaigne also uses travel to put his own culture into perspective. In Lindau he praises the 'well favoured' inn food, remarking 'that the kitchens of our French nobility would hardly appear to compare'. There they serve an abundance of fish, game, woodcock, and leveret, 'which they season in a manner very different to ours, but equally as good'. In Basel the metalworkers surpass their French counterparts, 'and no matter how small the church, they have a magnificent clock and sundial'. In Italy they sieve their flour with wheels, so that the baker does 'more work in an hour than we do in four'. And soon there emerges a slight disdain for his own country: 'against which he had a hatred and aversion for other reasons' (because of its religious wars), throwing himself wholeheartedly into foreign manners, even going 'so far as to drink his wine without water'. He concludes that the things he wished he had brought with him were: 'a cook, to be taught in their ways, and to be able to show proof of it at home'; secondly, a German valet, so that he wouldn't be swindled; and thirdly a proper guide book, such as Sebastian Münster's *Cosmographie Universelle* of 1544, a copy of which he acquires when he gets home.

Montaigne's interest in other cultures also extends beyond the shores of Europe. In Rome he becomes friendly with 'an old patriarch of Antioch, an Arab', who impresses him with his knowledge of 'five or six languages of those beyond' – i.e. from the Middle East. He gives Montaigne a medicine for his kidney stone in a 'little earthenware pot', Montaigne using his journal to record the prescription: after a light supper 'take about the size of two peas, diluted in warm water, having crumbled it with your fingers first'.

And Montaigne's open-mindedness is also to the fore when he visits a house in Rome to witness what he describes as 'the most ancient religious ceremony in existence among men' – the circumcision of a young Jewish boy. Here Montaigne's interest is palpable. His mother was possibly of Jewish descent, and he had earlier visited the synagogue in Verona 'and had a long talk with them about their ceremonies'. Whether Montaigne, a devout Catholic, is sympathetic to Judaism because of his mother's background is difficult to say. But what comes across is an even-handedness and an objectivity of description that is similar to his earlier description of a Lutheran wedding – leaving theology on the page and letting the actual practice of religion speak for itself:

> They pay no more attention to their prayers than we do to ours, talking of other matters at the same time, and not bringing much reverence to their mysteries . . . After dinner the doctors, in turn, give a lesson on the passage of the Bible for that day, doing it in Italian. After the lesson, some other doctor present selects one of the hearers, or sometimes two or three in succession, to argue against the one who has just been reading, on what he has said. The one we listened to seemed to have much eloquence and much wit in his argument.

He goes on to describe the circumcision, comparing it to aspects of Catholic ritual. The boy receives a godfather and a godmother 'as we do', and is swaddled 'after our fashion'. He describes how the *mohel* warms his hands, before cutting off the foreskin, and sucking the blood from the wound. There is 'a great deal of effort' in the procedure 'and some pain', records Montaigne. But he does not seem to pass judgement. The boy cries, but 'as ours do when they are baptized', but is soothed by being allowed to suck a finger dipped in wine.

But perhaps the most interesting example of Montaigne 'rubbing and polishing our brains with others' comes in his essay 'Of Cannibals', which he writes in the two years before he travels to Italy, but subsequently adds to in the years up to his death.

The sixteenth century saw a huge expansion of Atlantic trade, with ships setting off from France and Spain for the six-week voyage to the Americas, returning laden with silver, brazilwood and spices, and tales of unknown people, animals and natural phenomena, such as the yellow fruit called *paco* (bananas) and the toucan.

But this geographic expansion still represented a shock to European culture, which from antiquity had believed that God had ordained that there were only three continents – Europe, Africa and Asia – in line with the Father the Son and the Holy Ghost. Montaigne registers this shock and

awe, but also uses it to take his mind off the beaten track, to see how 'we should guard against holding on to vulgar opinions, and judge things by the light of reason, and not by common hearsay'.

Montaigne never travelled to the New World but he tells how he employed a man who had lived for ten or twelve years in what was called 'Antarctic France', or Brazil. The name would seem to presuppose a colonial arrogance, but Montaigne goes on to speculate presciently about the changes geology and oceanography have made to the face of the earth – cutting Sicily off from Italy, but perhaps also severing the ancient unity of Europe and the Americas, a view he supports by citing the changes in the course of the Dordogne during his own lifetime, and the sea's reclaiming of his brother's estate in the Médoc.

Aristotle too, he notes, relates how the Carthaginians discovered a large island in the Atlantic, 'all clothed in woods and watered by large, deep rivers', but were prohibited from settling by their rulers, who feared that Carthage would become depopulated, and that this new world would supplant and replace them as a result. Like the philosophical conundrum of the Ship of Theseus – where Theseus progressively replaces the rotten boards of his ship, to the extent that one might ask, is it the same ship as it was before? – Montaigne asks: if we are all in fact descended from the same land mass and are in fact all related (as palaeobiology now shows that we are), who is to say, therefore, who is civilized and who is not? Or who will be the civilized and uncivilized in ages to come?

Montaigne turns to his ex-servant, who unlike Aristotle 'was a simple and ignorant fellow' and much more likely to tell the truth, and who over the years had brought several traders and sailors to his house. And from what he hears, Montaigne flies in the face of popular opinion – which sees the inhabitants of the New World as barbaric – and charts his own point of view:

I can see nothing barbarous or savage about that nation, from what I have heard, other than that we call barbaric whatever does not fit in with our custom. Indeed, it seems that we have no other measure of truth and reason than the examples and ideas of the opinions and customs of the country in which we live. Here is always the perfect religion, the perfect government, the perfect and accomplished manner of all things. These men are wild in the same way in which we call wild the fruits that nature has produced by herself and in her ordinary course; whereas in truth it is those we have altered by our artifice and diverted from the common order that we should rather call wild.

It is therefore ourselves who are really barbaric, in corrupting and smothering Nature's beauty with clothing and decoration. By contrast, he remarks upon the uncultivated fruits of this new Eden: 'which possess a delicacy of flavour that is excellent to the taste and to the envy of our own'. Montaigne thus turns the tables, and inaugurates a tradition that culminates in Rousseau's idea of the noble savage – a prelapsarian state of nature more to be esteemed than artificial poise. And in his later essay 'Of Coaches', Montaigne places himself in the minds of the Amerindians, and looks back on himself and his own kind:

For, take away from those who subjugated them the tricks and artifices which they used to deceive them, and the natural astonishment of the people on seeing the unexpected arrival of bearded men, differing from them in language, religion, shape and countenance, from a faraway region of the world, where they had never imagined that there could be any habitation, mounted on big unknown monsters . . . men with a hard and shining skin and sharp and glittering weapons against men who, for the miracle of the gleam of a mirror or a knife would exchange great wealth in gold and pearls . . . add to this the thunder and the lightning of our cannon and arquebuses . . . against people who were naked . . . people taken by surprise, under colour of friendship and good faith, curious to see strange and unknown things. Take into account, I say, all the superiority of the conquerors, and you deprive them of all the credit of so many victories.

In contrast to the 'good faith' of the Amerindians, the conquistadors rely on deception and trickery. And Montaigne goes on to ponder how Plato would have been interested to meet these people: 'The very words that signify falsehood, treason, dissimulation, avarice, envy, detraction . . . unheard of!'

Montaigne goes on to furnish his own vision from anecdote: the wooden swords of the warriors, the cotton hammocks slung up in the male and female dorms. They are clean-shaven and wear bracelets and carry long hollow canes that they play to accompany their dances. Their morality consists of two simple commandments: to be valiant in war, and to love their wives.

And Montaigne directly addresses their supposed 'barbarity'. They go to war naked but fight with great courage, wishing only to display valour (they don't engage in war for something so petty as land). They treat prisoners well, ensuring they are afforded every kindness, before joining together with their best friends in killing, roasting and eating them, sending choice cuts to absent friends. But eating their enemies is not done for food, but simply as ritualized retribution. And Montaigne contrasts this with the Portuguese method of killing – of burying a man up to his waist, filling him with arrows and *then* hanging him. Montaigne thus excoriates the moral blindness of the Europeans' 'superiority':

> I think there is more barbarity in eating a living than a dead man, in tearing and torturing on the rack a body still full of feeling, in roasting slowly and giving him to be bitten and mangled by dogs and pigs (as we have not only read, but seen within recent memory, not between ancient enemies, but between neighbours and fellow citizens, and, what is worse, under the pretext of piety and religion), than in roasting and eating him after he is dead.

And it is here that Montaigne recalls the execution of the bandit Catena, when it was only the indignities heaped upon the dead man's body that seemed to arouse any pity or shock among the crowd.

But it would be wrong to see Montaigne as simply a cultural relativist, seeing cultures as necessarily sealed in their own moral double-glazing and playing them off against each other in some sort of intellectual game. For one of the most interesting aspects of the essay is Montaigne's sense of the parallels between the religion of the Amerindians and Christianity. One of the most frequently made accusations against Catholics by Protestants was that their view of the 'real presence' in the Eucharist made eating it effectively an act of cannibalism. Here Montaigne answers it by saying that more 'innocent' cultures engage in such acts, but do so in a more honest way. When not eating their enemies they live off bread and wine, a wine that is 'made of some root, and is of the colour of our claret wines', and a bread that is 'sweet and rather tasteless'. An everyday diet that is similar to communion bread and wine, only perhaps closer to the original: for 'they only drink it warm'. And this is the nurturing task of the women, in keeping the 'wine warm and seasoned'.

What therefore runs like a subterranean stream through the pages of the essay is the idea that all religion – Christian and Amerindian alike – is involved in a desire for contact with the other person's body, and through them oneself; a worship that, through sublimation and 'culture', Christianity has perverted and made the source of doubt and pointless cruelty. But what is the bone of contention in Christianity – the Eucharist – is a source of solidarity in its unadulterated form, even in the ritualized song that a prisoner sings to his captors:

> That they should come boldly, and assemble to dine off him: for they shall be eating their fathers and grandfathers, whose flesh has served to feed and nourish this body. These muscles, he says, this flesh and these veins are yours, poor fools that you are: can you not see that they still contain the substance of your ancestors' limbs? Savour them well, you will find that they have the taste of your own flesh.

These are words that echo the consecration of the host: 'this is my body', 'this is my blood'. But what is important is that the Amerindian version also contains the source of its own moderation. The description of their revenge thus amounts to a process of personal and bodily reintegration – literally, incorporation – not only among the victors, but also between the victors and the victims, who have themselves dined on their enemies' ancestors. The act of ingestion thus becomes mutual: in the act of eating, they are eaten, and themselves eat themselves. What Montaigne emphasizes is the relishing and tasting of the body, to such an extent that the two fleshes become consubstantial: 'the taste of your own flesh'. Through the sampling of another's being they sample their own, and religiously and philosophically touch – and *taste* – base.

But what is perhaps most important for Montaigne is that the *savouring* of this fact serves to satisfy and therefore moderate their appetite – it is this ritual aspect rather than the quantity of flesh that *nourishes* them (to use one of Montaigne's favourite words – *nourrir*). And this ability to actively, consciously taste and savour, and hence be nourished, is at the heart of the difference between the Amerindians and Europeans for Montaigne. They eat meat and fish 'roasted without any other preparation' and eat on first rising, the one meal satisfying them for the rest of the day. Their wine is a laxative to those who are not used to it (i.e. it has the opposite effect of incorporation), but to them it is good for the stomach and 'very pleasant'. As a result of this proper satedness, they do not prospect beyond the bounds of what nature has laid out for them and live a life that stands as an inversion of consumer consumption, a vision of the original Amerindian dream:

> They do not struggle to conquer new territory, for they still enjoy that luxuriance that nature provides for them, without labour and pains, with all necessary things in such abundance, that they have no need to aggrandize

their borders. They are still in that happy state of not desiring more than their natural necessities demand: anything beyond that is superfluous for them.

And it is this lack of bodily nourishment that lies at the heart of the bloodthirsty cruelty of the Europeans. The Amerindians have no need for torture or extortion: 'they ask of their prisoners no other ransom but a confession and acknowledgement of being conquered'. Their appetites are healthy, but not out of control. The idea of sinfulness seems to be unknown. Montaigne transcribes a song about a snake whose beautiful pattern is copied onto a girdle as a gift for a lover: 'Adder stay, stay adder, that my sister may use your colours as a pattern to fashion a rich girdle to give to my love.' In contrast to the Christian tradition, the serpent is a symbol of beauty and fidelity rather than sexual temptation, the girdle perhaps symbolizing chastity. Montaigne goes on to describe their language as 'soft', agreeable to the ear, 'something like Greek in its endings'.

Of course, Montaigne never visited South America, and all his knowledge is from secondary, anecdotal accounts, so we cannot draw any real anthropological or historical knowledge from it. 'Of Cannibals' is an imaginative 'essay' which mingles travel narratives, sailors' anecdotes and apocryphal tales from the New World to ponder issues that are really Montaigne's own. And yet, like his thoughts about animals, it allows him to explore an alternative reality, where men – even enemies – are united by religion rather than divided by it, and through it manifest a desire – albeit a cannibalistic one, but not a cruel one – for each other.

And here we can see the way in which these thoughts on cannibals inform his description of the 'most ancient religious ceremony' of circumcision that he witnesses in Rome. There the *mohel* takes some wine into his mouth and 'sucks the still bleeding glans of the boy and spits out the blood he has drawn from it'. This he does three times. He then dips his finger in the bloody glass and gives it to the boy to suck. The *mohel* then passes the glass 'in the same state' – i.e. still bloody – to the mother and the other women present 'to drink up the remainder'. They finish off by inhaling some incense from a vessel that Montaigne likens to a cassoulet – a cooking pot. What Montaigne emphasizes is a similarly ordered economy of body and blood exchange, from rabbi to boy, from boy to mother and then to the other women, and finally from the boy to himself, who is given a bloody, wine-dipped finger to suck, giving him 'the taste' of his 'own flesh'. Whether Montaigne approves of all this is impossible to say – in a later aside he describes circumcision as a punishment for sex. But what is interesting is that the next entry in the journal describes the 'licentiousness' of the Christian Shrovetide celebrations, where naked old men and Jews are made to race against each other and are humiliated. And carnival, as Montaigne well knew, constitutes a farewell to the flesh before the onset of Lent – *carne-vale*.

At the end of his essay 'Of Cannibals', Montaigne reveals how he came across three Tupinamba Indians after the siege of Rouen in 1562 (Rouen enjoyed a monopoly on the importation of brazilwood from the New World). Just like he asks of his cat, Montaigne is interested in the question: What do they think of us? Tantalizingly, Montaigne says that he could remember only two of the three things they said. Firstly, they said that they wondered why so many men with big beards were ruled by a child (Charles IX was only twelve at the time). And:

Secondly (they have a way of speaking of men as 'halves' of one another), that they had observed that they had seen men amongst us, full and gorged with all kinds of things, and that their halves were begging at their doors, emaciated with hunger and poverty.

Montaigne then managed to speak to one of them alone, and asked what he gained from his status (he was the equivalent of a captain). He responded that he was allowed to lead from the front during war. But what about in peacetime? Then, he said, the villagers under his rule would clear paths through the undergrowth, so that he might gain access to their village more easily.

Montaigne then finishes with an ironic flourish: 'This is all very well, but hang on, they don't even wear trousers' – meaning that we will forever judge others by our own habitual prejudices. But this sense of honour as manifested in an openness to the other person, in a gesture of welcoming them and meeting them half-way, is something that seems to strike a certain chord with Montaigne.

The highlight of his stay in Rome is his meeting with the Pope – *Pontifex Maximus, Episcopus Ecclesiae Catholicae* – his secretary making a note of the elaborate choreography required in venerating God's plenipotentiary on earth, but at the end of the day, a man of flesh, and blood – and feet:

It is true that most people do not go straight towards him, cutting across the room, instead shuffling a little along the wall, and, after this detour, make straight for him. When they are half-way they again go down on one knee, and receive the second benediction. This done, they go towards him as far as a velvet carpet spread out at his feet, seven or eight feet further. At the edge of this carpet they get down on both knees. The ambassador presenting them then got down on one knee, and turned back the Pope's robe from the right foot, on which there is a red slipper with a white cross upon it. Those who are on their knees drag themselves along in this posture up to his foot, and stoop down to the ground to kiss it. Monsieur de Montaigne said that he had slightly raised the end of his toe.

8

The Philosopher's Stone

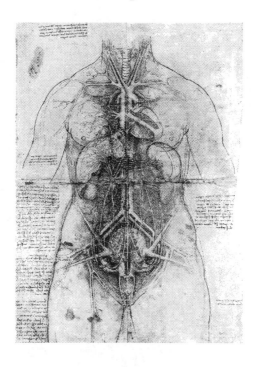

A few months later Montaigne found himself in slightly less formal surroundings, relaxing trouserlessly in the warm mineral baths at Bagni di Lucca. The final goal of his travels was to sample the thermal baths of Italy – drinking and bathing in them – as a treatment for the kidney stones that had plagued him over the past few years, and in April 1581 Montaigne set off from Rome for the baths in high spirits. Upon arriving, he inspected the rooms on offer before splashing out on the finest one available:

> especially for the view, which commands . . . the whole of the little valley and the River Lima, and the mountains which shelter the same valley, all well-cultivated and green to the summit, filled with chestnut and olive trees and elsewhere with vines, that they plant all over the mountains and arrange in circles and terraces . . . From my room all night I listen to the gentle sound of the river.

He has a dining room, three bedrooms and a kitchen, and a fresh napkin every day, which he uses to clean his teeth. And he sets about taking the waters, bathing in a dark vaulted pool about half the size of his dining room at Montaigne, and recording in his journal the quantities of fluids in and fluids out. He even has a go with something called a *doccia*, from which 'you receive hot water upon different parts of the body, and especially the head . . . in a continual spray'.

Spread around the mountainside are other baths, all having their own therapeutic powers: 'One cools, another warms, this one for one illness, that one for another, and thereabouts a thousand miracles; in short, there is no kind of illness that does not find its cure there.'

Montaigne's kidney stones had a profound effect upon his life. Seeing his father being 'grievously tormented' and fainting with pain in the seven years before his death contributed to his initial pessimism. He began to suffer in his kidneys about the time he was forty, not long after his retirement, but the stone's full force struck him at forty-five, two years before he published his first edition of the *Essays*, plaguing him with its capricious misery. Of the surprises that life held in store, he wished that fate had allocated him something different: 'For he could not have chosen one of which I have had a greater horror since childhood . . . it is the one I dreaded most.' So when Montaigne first published the *Essays* in 1580, he could be forgiven for thinking that he had only five years left to live – another reason to travel to see the world: to literally see Rome and die.

Kidney stones (renal calculi) are most commonly formed from calcium oxalate crystals that occur in the urine and are deposited in the kidney in too great a quantity to disperse. Diet may be a cause, but a key factor is genetic predisposition, and Montaigne wonders why he had been bequeathed this hereditary time-bomb. He was conceived before his father suffered from the stone and he asks how, out of the small drop of sperm from which he was constructed, the knowledge of his future had been ordained. And why did he alone out his brothers and sisters suffer in this fashion?

It is, Montaigne says, 'the most sudden, the most painful, the most fatal and most incurable of all diseases', the symptoms occurring when larger stones become stuck in the urinary tract causing vomiting, fever and excruciating pain. He notes in his essay 'Of Suicide' Pliny's observation that it is the disease most likely to make men kill themselves, and wishes he could have the luck of the man mentioned by Cicero, who, having a wet dream, discharged a stone into his sheets. In contrast, he says, his curiously 'unwench' him, and diminish his natural get-up-and-go.

And the suffering can be prolonged. In Rome just before Christmas he spends the night passing gravel and a stone that took six hours to travel through his penis. His travels are interrupted by days of immobility, which vexes Montaigne – for whom life is nothing if not movement – almost as much as the pain.

But on the condition and its management Montaigne considers himself something of an expert. He takes a keen interest in treatments and cures, and consults the latest papers on mineral therapies – Bacci's *De thermis* (1571), Donati's *De acquis lucensibus* (1580). And he is flattered when at the baths some medical men call on him to ask for a second opinion. But, in truth, the sixteenth-century body was still a mysterious codex that had yet to be properly unrolled. One gentleman swears by the medicinal effects of a mysterious green gemstone carried about him, obtained from a monk who had travelled in India. In Baden, they believe in the curative powers of bathing after scarifying, soaking in waters turned incarnadine with blood. The Cremona merchant with dementia tells Montaigne how he is perplexed by the behaviour of his flatulence, how it rushes out of his ears during the night. He advises Montaigne that the best way to get the bowels moving is to moisten some coriander seeds in one's mouth and then insert them into one's anus (important to remember which way round). Montaigne tries, but is deflated at the outcome: 'a lot of wind, of which I was quite full; of matter, little'.

Montaigne therefore resorts to his own dispensations. He takes short showers, and bathes and drinks and bathes again, shocking local opinion. He puts his groin under the water spout and feels, as he thinks, the wind escaping from his genitals, his right testicle slowly going down. And in the progress of the stone he witnesses the mysteries of microcosm and macrocosm, the larger being recapitulated by the small:

> On the 24th, in the morning, I passed a stone which stopped in the passage. From that moment until dinner I held back my urine, to increase the urge. Then, not without pain and blood, both before and after, I passed it. It was of the size and length of a pine-nut, but big at one end like a bean. To tell the truth, it was exactly the same shape as a prick.

He wonders what will follow. And he varies his treatment to try and second guess his illness. He bathes, drinks five pounds of water and goes on an invigorating two-mile walk; but again to no avail – 'farted endlessly'.

One evening the pain of trapped wind is so unbearable that he calls for Captain Paulino, who, like many proprietors at the baths, doubles as a complementary therapist. He requests an enema, almost as one might order a cocktail from the lounge-bar of a luxury five-star hotel:

> which was very comfortably administered to me at sundown, made of oil, chamomile and aniseed, and nothing else, according to the prescription of the apothecary alone. Captain Paulino delivered it to me with such skill that, feeling the wind rushing out against

it, he stopped and drew back, and then continued very gradually so that I absorbed the whole thing without trouble. He did not need to remind me to retain it as long as I could, for it did not move my bowels at all. I was in this state for three hours, and then tried by myself to void it.

But the general prognosis is not good. Generally, drinking water is beneficial for kidney stones, in that it dilutes the urine, separating the calcium crystals, and Montaigne observes others whose health does seem restored. But he himself continues to suffer, and the heavy draughts of water seem to bring on other complications: he gets a toothache (which the doctor puts down to flatulence), and migraines which affect his sight. He tries to bathe his eyes, dunking his head in the water, but 'felt no effect from it, either good or bad'. He becomes increasingly aware of the disagreements in medical opinion: Donati saying that that it is better to eat little and drink more, Franciotti saying the opposite. 'What a vain thing is medicine!' exclaims Montaigne: 'It is a stupid habit to measure how much you piss.' And towards the end of his stay he begins to feel that the waters may be the source as much as the solution to his problems:

> For myself, if I judge correctly about these waters, they do neither much harm nor much good; they are weak and insipid stuff, and it is to be feared that they heat the kidneys more than they purge them.

And at the beginning of September 1581 he 'began to find these baths unpleasant'. He falls into a melancholy mood, not dissimilar to that that which he experienced upon first arriving, when he recalled the memory of his friend:

when writing to Monsieur d'Ossat, I fell into such distressing thoughts about Monsieur de La Boétie, and felt like that for so long, without recovering, that it caused me much pain.

He speaks to a local man, who says that the baths have killed more than they have healed, and on the night of 4 September Montaigne reaches rock bottom, the agony of toothache augmenting the pain of the stone. It attacks his jaw, spreading to his head, such that he sweats and shivers and is incapable of standing. In the middle of the night he calls for Captain Paulino, who prescribes *aqua vitae* (ethanol) which gives him some relief when he holds it in his mouth. But as he drifts off into sleep, exhausted, it trickles down his throat, causing him to choke. 'It was', he says, 'the cruellest night I ever remember having spent.'

❧

But in the face of this suffering, the baths bring other benefits, ones that work on the spirit as much as anything else. For the next day, as he lies cradling his aching jaw, Montaigne records a rather touching scene:

> On the Tuesday morning all the gentlemen who were at the baths came to see me in bed. I had a small mastic plaster put on the pulse on my left temple. On this day I suffered little. At night they put a hot poultice on the cheek and the left side of my head. I slept free from pain . . .

It is curiously affecting to see this sixteenth-century nobleman, a scion of the nobility of the sword, a student of the Stoic strictures of the ancients, being solicitously visited in his sickbed by his fellow noblemen because of a toothache. And at the baths Montaigne finds society, companionship – one might even say friends. His fellow-bathers spoil him with wine and provisions. He visits the village of Menabbio where he dines with Signor Santo, a wealthy soldier, taking with him a gift of fish. And back at the baths he is invited out for an evening, to a ball:

> where several gentlewomen were gathered, well dressed but of ordinary beauty, although they were among the best looking of Lucca. In the evening Signor Ludovico de Ferrari of Cremona, whom I know well, sent me a present of some boxes of very good quince jelly, scented, and some limes, and some oranges of an extraordinary size.

Moreover, on returning to the baths for a second visit after an excursion to Florence, he experiences a reception similar to that which he would hope to receive at Montaigne:

> Great were the welcomes and caresses I received from all these people. Indeed, I might have thought I had returned to my own house. I took up the same room that I had the first time, at a price of twenty scudi a month, and on the same terms.

And he goes off for his first dip of the morning 'not only healthy, but in all round good spirits'.

Companionship thus helps to take Montaigne out of himself. But it has to be said that this bonhomie is also helped by the rather relaxed, sexy ambience of the baths. At the beginning of his trip Montaigne copies down the rules on the walls of the bathhouse at Plombières. They state that not only is it forbidden to swear, quarrel, bear arms or give the lie, but also:

> All prostitutes and immodest girls are forbidden to enter the said baths, or to approach the same within five hundred paces . . . [and] all persons are forbidden to use towards the ladies, gentlewomen and other women and girls, frequenting the said baths, any lascivious or immodest language; to touch their persons indecorously; or to enter or quit the said baths disrespectfully, contrary to public propriety . . .

One is reminded of those signs on public swimming pools that outlawed 'acrobatics, gymnastics, diving' but also, rather quaintly, 'smoking and petting'. Montaigne copies the entire proclamation down at great length.

But in its rather officious tone, it could be said that the sign perhaps protests a little too much. For in a contemporary guide to the same baths, Jean Le Bon's *Short Description of the Properties of the Baths of Plombières* (1576), we see a different picture, mingling propriety with a slightly more titillating undertone:

> On the morning that you take a bath, the man enters with culottes or pants, the women with a blouse of fairly thick cloth (too much undone reveals that which the bath does not wish to see). One bathes pell-mell, as some play instruments, some eat, some doze, others dance in such a way that the company is never bored, and never feels time beginning to drag.

And in a Renaissance painting of the baths at Bourbon l'Archambaut, things seem to be getting a little steamy. In

their defence, it has to be said that the baths at Bagni di Lucca
did have a separate area for women. But the policing of such
divisions is obviously rather lax, as Montaigne himself goes
and bathes in the women's section one morning, and quotes
a local rhyme suggesting that such divisions can never really
overcome the attraction of the sexes:

> *Chi vuol che la sua donna impregni,*
> *Mandila al bagno, e non ci vengi.*

> If you want your wife impregnated,
> Take her to the baths and then vacate it.

And clearly Montaigne is rather an unreconstructed man
in his attitude towards women. In Rome, 'as at Paris', he
takes a keen interest in the local prostitutes and finds 'the
most remarkable beauty . . . among those who put it up for
sale'. In Venice the celebrated *meretrice* Veronica Franca even
sends Montaigne some examples of her verse. He admires the
ladies of Ancona, who are famed for their beauty, although

in Fano, a town also renowned for its beautiful women, he is disappointed: 'We saw none, but some very ugly ones, and when I asked an honest man of the town, he told me that that was a long time ago.'

If there was a place to indulge his taste in women, though, it was at the baths. After dinner on a Sunday in May he holds a ball for the 'peasant girls' which is so successful that he holds another, this time inviting the gentlemen and the ladies who are also resident, and holding a competition to find the best dancers. He sends to Lucca for the prizes: for the men a leather belt and a bonnet of black cloth; for the ladies two muslin and two taffeta aprons, one green, one violet, four papers of pins, a pair of slippers, three crystal nets, three braids of hair, four little necklaces and four pairs of pumps (although he gives one of these to a girl not at the ball). The prizes are tied to a hoop for all to see.

Montaigne clearly enjoys himself, expressing his characteristic open-mindedness with a certain raffish charm:

> In truth, it is a beautiful thing, and a rare one to us French, to see these peasant girls, so graceful and dressed like ladies, dancing so well: in this they could compete with the rarest of our ladies . . .

At the end of the evening he addresses the party and requests the help of the ladies in awarding the prizes. They politely decline out of courtesy and at last he agrees to distribute them, mingling chivalry with a certain *droit de seigneur*:

> I did in fact go about choosing with my eyes, now one, now the other, and always with regard to their beauty and gentleness, pointing out that the charm of the dance did not depend solely in the movement of the feet, but

also the countenance, bearing, but also the carriage and elegance of the whole body. The prizes were distributed, more to some, less to others, according to their value . . . It was all conducted in an orderly and regular manner, except that one of the girls refused the prize. She begged me, for her sake, to give it to another, which I did not think was the right thing to do. She was not one of the most attractive.

Whether Montaigne exploits his *droit de seigneur* more fully is difficult to say. It is perhaps significant that on the morning after the ball he arrives 'a little later at the bath', after stopping to get a haircut and a shave. On the other hand, he seems to miss his family, his wife and his daughter, having a plaque to them placed on the walls of the shrine of Our Lady of Loreto, showing them kneeling before the figure of Mary, accompanied by the inscription: 'Michel de Montaigne, Gascon Frenchman, Knight of the Order of the King, 1581, Françoise de La Chassaigne, his wife, and Léonor de Montaigne, his only daughter.'

But what is most important about Montaigne's stay at the baths and the pleasures – sexual or not – that they bring, is that it creates in him an acute awareness of his body. With other illnesses, he notes, as soon as you are returned to 'fresh air, and wine and your wife and melons' (his favourite fruit), 'it is a wonder if you do not relapse into some new misery'. But the stone 'takes itself off clean', focusing his attention on painlessness as well as pain. The stone therefore offers a way of becoming aware of health, of what it is to *be*. Through it Montaigne achieves an intensification of his kinaesthetic sense of himself, of being Michel de Montaigne. The sensation of ejecting a stone he thus celebrates in terms which echo both birth and sexual climax:

> . . . is there anything sweeter than the sudden change when, after extreme pain, by ejecting the stone I recover, in a flash of lightning, the beautiful light of health, so free and so full, as happens after our sudden and sharpest attacks of colic? Can the pain we have suffered for a moment counterbalance the pleasure of such a sudden recovery? How much more beautiful health appears to me after the illness, when they come so close and are in such close contact, that I am able to recognize them in their full armour; when they appear as two opponents testing and defying one another.

In these intervals when 'my ureters are languid without stinging' Montaigne says he returns to his 'natural state . . . I talk, I laugh, I study.' And writing towards the end of his days, he has 'flashes of recovery so clear, though irregular and brief, that they fall little short of my youthful health and freedom from pain'. The role of pain becomes transformed, not as something with which to hone our Stoic indifference to life, but something to bring our sense of life closer:

> Just as the Stoics say that vices have been introduced as an aid to virtue, we may say, with better reason and less bold conjecture, that nature has given us pain in order to honour and appreciate pleasure and relaxation.

Warm water, wine, and melons, and the subtle smile of a pretty girl's eyes: all have the power to improve Montaigne's mood. But simple painlessness, 'the beautiful light of health' –

'a bubbling, rich, and lazy health' – has a transformative power.

But what is equally important is how suffering facilitates companionship and fellow feeling for Montaigne. In his final essay he says with unabashed snobbery: 'I see on all hands men afflicted with the same sort of illness, and it is an honourable society, since it attaches itself by preference to the great: it is essentially a noble and dignified disease.' He writes to Marshal de Matignon with a fellow sufferer's bonhomie, wishing that 'the stone that was troubling you lately . . . has now slipped out easily, like the one that I expelled at the same time'. The Seigneur de Langon even demonstrates how to stop the flow of urine and turn it on again, so that the stone may pop out like a cork. (Little wonder Montaigne is so obsessed with waterworks and fountains and their carefree *jouissance*.)

The stone also exposes Montaigne to simple kindness. He says how he has swallowed 'broths of eryngo or rupture wort' numerous times 'to please the ladies, who with a kindness greater than the sharpness of my pain, offered me half of theirs'. And summarizing his findings after his return from his travels, he concludes that the value of bathing lies in the company as much as in the waters themselves:

> He who does not bring with him so much cheerfulness so as to enable him to enjoy the pleasure of the society he will meet there, and the walks and exercise to which the beauty of the places in which these waters are commonly located invites us, will doubtless lose the best and greatest part of their effect.

And so Montaigne's journey comes to an end. The cure he had hoped to find fails to materialize – in his final essay he writes that only 'fools' believe that stones are to be dissolved 'by drinking' – but a deeper restoration has taken place. For Montaigne, travel makes a man a foreigner unto himself, not only in his manners, language, and customs, but in his habitual sense of his self. Through it, he begins to consider the distinction between sameness and difference, barbarism and civilization, concluding that what is often seen as uncivilized is simply 'off the hinges of custom'. He says that he looks upon 'all men as my countrymen and embraces a Pole as I would a Frenchman'. Moreover, in opening ourselves to other customs and other people, travel has the power to revitalize our relationship to ourselves, in the intermixture of our mind and body, of ourselves and ourself.

On 7 September 1581, after soaking for an hour in the bath at Lucca, Montaigne receives the letter he had feared, informing him of his election to the mayoralty of Bordeaux, urging him to accept 'for the love of my country'. Duty calls. He returns home in a rather circumambulatory manner, however, by way of Siena and Rome, telling his secretary that he sees himself 'like a person who is reading some amusing story or a fine book and begins to be afraid that he is getting towards the end'. But as he does eventually reach his destination, nearly three months later, his narration carries on:

> On Sunday, 26th of November, I left Limoges after dinner, and went to sleep at
> LES CARS, five leagues, where there was no-one but Madame des Cars. On the Monday I came to sleep at
> PÉRIGUEUX, five leagues. On the Wednesday to sleep at
> MAURIAC, five leagues. On the Thursday, St Andrew's Day, the last day of November, to sleep at
> MONTAIGNE, seven leagues, which I had left on the 22nd

June 1580, to go to La Fère. Thus my travels had taken seventeen months and eight days.

'To sleep at Montaigne.' What is interesting is how Montaigne portrays his homecoming as if it were another stop on the way: staying with himself, as it were; granting himself the honour of sleeping in his own bed. And as if to witness this discreet moment of self-meeting, he goes up to his library and re-records it in the flyleaves of his copy of Beuther's *Ephemeris Historica*, turning his diary into a guest book, pressing within its pages the silent movements of his own hand.

9

The Exercises of Venus

The return from his travels inaugurated a sustained period of public service for Montaigne, serving as mayor for two terms in the years from 1581 to 1585. His reluctance to take up the post was no doubt influenced by the image he drew of his father during his own mayoralty: 'I remember seeing him as a boy ... with little regard to his own life, which he came near to losing, obliged as he was to make long and laborious journeys on their behalf.' And for Montaigne these were even more troubling times, with him attempting to negotiate between the Catholic forces loyal to the King and the competing interests of the Protestant leader Henri de Navarre. He says that some objected that his administration passed without leaving a 'mark or a trace', but responds: 'I am accused of doing nothing when almost everyone else was guilty of doing too much!'

But somehow Montaigne managed to find time to return to the *Essays*. Newly amended editions were issued in 1582 and 1587, and in 1588 a new enlarged edition was published, including significant additions to the text and a third volume of thirteen new essays. (Montaigne's own copy of this edition, with his further handwritten additions, still survives, being known as the 'Bordeaux copy' and which serves as the basis for most modern editions of his text.) In these later expansions Montaigne bears out his statement that 'The Mayor and Montaigne have always been two' by writing in a more personal tone, composing essays on subjects such as vanity, repentance, and sex.

In himself Montaigne represents the other-worldliness of Renaissance attitudes to sex, being at once more strait-laced but more unbridled than we are. His wife was twenty when she married the thirty-two-year-old Montaigne, and was supposedly quite beautiful, but Montaigne nevertheless conducted himself with reserve in the marital bed. He compares himself to Maximilian I of Austria, who, despite great physical beauty, was as 'careful as a virgin in not revealing himself, even writing in his will that they should put underpants on him when he had died'. And one of Montaigne's friends, Florimond de Raemond, annotates his own copy of the *Essays* with a note about Montaigne's marital chastity, stating that he had not even glimpsed his wife's breasts. But Montaigne seems to unbutton in his essays, whose freedom allows him to call into question 'those comical inhibitions by which our society is so fettered'.

For, central to the Stoic and the Christian morality of his time was a shared antipathy towards sex. The Christian story began with Satan's temptation of Eve, and Eve's subsequent temptation of Adam, linking original sin with women. But the Stoics also saw sex as disabling through its association with women, and their softening and weakening effect. Zeno, the founder of the Stoic sect, had relations with a woman only once, notes Montaigne, and this was merely to save face. And in his *De Constantia*, Justus Lipsius describes the heaven of a male-only Garden of Eden, untroubled by the emotional demands of the weaker vessel. Such misogynistic attitudes were repeated on a popular level, where women were seen as fickle and inconstant, their bodies mysteriously leaky through their monthly cycles, the vagina a dark and terrifyingly unknowable place. *Diaboli virtus in lumbis est*, as St Jerome said: 'The power of the devil is in the loins.'

The religious response to the body was thus one of

chastisement, as Montaigne says – 'vigils, fasts, and hair-shirts, distant and solitary exiles, perpetual imprisonments, scourges, and other afflictions' – a process he himself witnessed in Rome, where a procession of penitents scarified their shoulders, their whips 'so clotted with gore that they had to be wetted before they could be unwound'. And whilst a popular ribaldry continued through the sixteenth century, the latter half saw an increasing repression of sexual mores. Bedrooms became separated from living areas, and children made to sleep on their own. Underpants became obligatory and nakedness taboo. Words referring to particular parts of the body also came to be seen as dirty – 'we dare not call our members by their right name,' complains Montaigne. And a stream of conduct manuals placed an increasing emphasis on policing sexual behaviour, particularly in terms of the chastity of daughters and wives. In his widely read *The Christian State of Matrimony* (1541) the Swiss reformer Henry Bullinger described 'how daughters and maidens must be kept':

> As for this thing every discreet parent shall know by the foresaid rules how to order them to avoid all wantonness . . . Books of Robin Hood, Beves of Hampton, Troilus and such like fables do but kindle in liars like lies and wanton love, which ought not in youth with their first spittle to be drunk in . . . Take the New Testament in your hands and study it diligently, and learn your profession in baptism to mortify your flesh . . .

Against these paranoid strictures Montaigne strikes a more reasonable tone. He recalls how his own daughter whilst reading stumbled across the word '*fouteau*' (beech), pronouncing it '*foutre*' (fuck), which caused her tutor some momentary discomfiture.

But this Montaigne records as a more worldly, unshockable observer, noting how her tutor's embarrassment served only to arouse his daughter's interest. And this puritanical context is reflected in the coy indirection of the title of Montaigne's essay on sex: 'On Some Verses of Virgil'.

But as Montaigne embarks on these later essays, at the age of fifty-three, he grows more indiscreet as he grows more mature, franker in his confessions, signalling his rejection of the strictures of Stoicism, and polite society, and his desire to:

> now deliberately allow myself a little licence, and sometimes occupy my mind, to give it a rest, with frisky and youthful thoughts. I am at this age too stale, too heavy and too mature. Every day my years read me lessons in coldness and temperance . . . It does not leave me an hour of respite, sleeping or waking, from preaching to me about death, patience, and penitence. I now defend myself against temperance, as I once did against sensuality.

Now he feels little by way of embarrassment and declares an urge to confess all: 'I speak truth, not as much as I would like, but as much as I dare; and I dare a little more as I grow older.'

He says he finds 'sweetness in the company of *beautiful and* honest women' (adding 'beautiful' at a later date) and recalls the tender age of his first sexual encounter – 'long before the age of choice and knowledge'. He boasts that in his early manhood he gave free rein to 'the fluttering wings of cupid', although does not recall managing more than six lovemakings in one assignation. He recalls how his whiskers served as a forget-me-not: 'the close kisses of youth, savory, greedy and sticky, used to cling to it and stay there for several hours', betraying 'the place I come from'. He asks to be dragged through the years backward, looking fondly on the sexual pleasures of his prime.

He says how he prefers 'wit rather than prudence' at the dinner table and 'beauty before goodness' in bed. He does not desire 'noble, magnificent and lofty' pleasures, so much as ones that are 'delicious, easy, and ready to hand'. He sees sex as principally a matter of 'sight and touch': 'one can do something without the charms of the mind, but nothing without the charms of the body'. He discusses ways to procrastinate ejaculation: 'to cast our soul back to other thoughts at this very instant' – perhaps to War Horses, or Whether a Ruler Should Go Out to Parley? But one must 'tense and stiffen it attentively', Montaigne advises – adding proudly in his final edition: 'I am well versed in this.'

Yet he pities his penis, saying that nature has 'done me the most enormous damage' in making it so small. And he confesses to episodes of impotence – 'an accident with which I am not unacquainted' – only to cross it out (twice, using different pens). Yet he talks about these 'ligatures', as they were often called, as natural failings, often resulting from the power of the imagination rather than witchcraft, as was often believed. He thus talks about a 'friend' (himself?) who suddenly suffered from this failing – 'in the very lap of enjoyment' – to the extent that the memory of it continually 'inhibited and tyrannized him'. He found relief in unburdening himself to another, which 'relieved the tension of his soul'. Are the essays, one wonders, Montaigne's own form of 'talking cure'?

And if things go wrong, Montaigne offers sympathetic counselling for sexual strife. Sex should not be rushed, nor attempted if unprepared. Men should attempt 'essays' and sallies, presenting themselves 'lightly' rather than risking a first refusal, with the result that sex becomes an issue.

Men also suffer though the unruliness of their penis, 'obtruding so rudely when we have no use for it and failing so importunately when we have most use for it . . . refusing with so much stubbornness and pride our solicitations, both mental and manual'. The former magistrate Montaigne puts his cock in the dock in a mock trial, but pleads the common insubordination of our other parts: the face that betrays our emotions; our hair standing on end. It is only penis-envy on their part that raises the accusing finger.

And once again Montaigne harks back to the ancients, but this time not for their fortitude and military strength, but for their relaxed attitude towards the body. He tells how they used a sponge to wipe themselves on the toilet, and cleaned themselves after sex using perfumed wool. Caesar had his body shaved and anointed with oil. He admires the Greek philosopher caught with his pants down who explained 'I am planting a man' as coolly as if he had been planting garlic. When caught masturbating in public, Diogenes quipped to onlookers that he wished that he could placate his stomach by rubbing it in the same way.

Their literature is similarly uninhibited, Montaigne listing the ancient works devoted to the art of love: Strato's *Of Carnal Conjunction*; Theophrastus' *The Lover* and *Of Love*; Aristippus' *Of Ancient Delights*; Aristo's *On Amorous Exercises*; not least Chrysippus' fable of Jupiter and Juno – 'shameless beyond all limits'. But most of all Montaigne admires the brazenness of their poetry, the verses of Virgil alluded to in his title telling how Venus (here in Dryden's translation):

. . . her arms, of snowy hue,
About her unresolving husband threw.
Her soft embraces soon infuse desire;
His bones and marrow sudden warmth inspire;
And all the godhead feels the wonted fire.
Not half so swift the rattling thunder flies,
Or forky lightnings flash along the skies . . .
Trembling he spoke; and, eager of her charms,
He snatch'd the willing goddess to his arms;
Till in her lap infus'd, he lay possess'd
Of full desire, and sunk to pleasing rest.

Ovid declaring even more flagrantly:

Et nudam pressi corpus ad usque meum.
I pressed her naked body close to mine.

'I feel he makes a eunuch of me with this expression . . . in exposing her so completely', confesses Montaigne.

In the 'Apology' Montaigne turns his attention to sperm, pondering the extrapolations of the ancients. Is it the froth of the best of our blood, as Pythagoras says, or the marrow from our backbone, as according to Plato it is here that we first begin to ache during sex? Is it part of the substance of the brain since those who are sex-addicted have eyes that are curiously bedimmed? Or is it distilled from the whole mass of the body, or rather both the soul and the body according to Epicurus? And is Creation itself little more than an enormous emission, as Socrates imagined, all life formed from a milky substance in what can only be called the original big bang?

And in his essayistic excursions upon the customs of the world, Montaigne free-associates about the liberal customs of other, unspecified places: where chastity is only prized in wedlock, and maidens abandon themselves at their leisure, securing abortions when pregnant with the use of drugs. In some places, tradesmen share their wives on their wedding night with their fellow workers, as do officers of higher rank. If it is the marriage of a labourer or peasant, she is presented to the local lord, notes Montaigne.

But, most of all, sex reveals our indebtedness to our bodies, showing that our body has a life and desires that overrule our Stoic decrees:

> The same cause that animates this member also animates, without our knowledge, the heart, the lungs and the pulse; the sight of a pleasing object spreads in us imperceptibly the flame of a feverish emotion . . . We do not command our hair to stand on end or our skin to shiver with desire or fear. The hand often moves itself to where we do not send it. The tongue is paralysed, and the voice is congealed, in their own time.

Orgasm itself shows the necessary confusion of mind and body – the moment when 'Venus prepares to sow the woman's fields' (Lucretius) and 'pleasure transports us so far beyond ourselves that our reason could not possibly then discharge its function, being all crippled and enraptured in pleasure'.

Nature, Montaigne notes, also likes to take a walk on the wild side.

Visiting Vitry-le-François on the Marne during his journey to Rome in 1580, Montaigne hears what he describes as 'three memorable stories'. The first is that the widow of the Duc de

Guise was still alive at the age of eighty-seven and still able to walk a mile. The second is that a few years previously a handful of local girls had taken upon themselves to dress as men and live their lives as such. One, named Mary, came to Vitry and earned her living as a weaver. She took up with a local girl but then broke off the relationship, moving to Montirandet. There she married a woman with whom she lived to her 'satisfaction' for four or five months, until she was recognized by a person from Chaumont and being brought before a justice she was condemned to be hanged – 'which she said she would rather endure than re-assume her original dress and habits'.

The third story concerns a man still living who until the age of twenty-two had been a girl named Marie – that is, until she leapt a ditch whilst chasing a pig and her 'masculine organs came forth'. Henceforth, local girls would sing a song warning about the dangers of putting a spring in their stride and thereby becoming a man. S/he was renamed Germain by the Bishop of Châlons (the name conveniently containing the former 'Marie') and was now heavily bearded, but living alone. Montaigne tried to pay a visit, but Germain was out.

There is clearly something in the water around Vitry, which was itself built as a replacement for 'the other Vitry', burnt down by Charles V some forty years before. But in these three memorable stories – of a widow in her virility making up for the loss of her husband, of two women living as man and wife, of a man born female – Montaigne touches on some of the deeper differences between modern and pre-modern notions of sexual difference, which makes the Renaissance worldview at once stranger but also more modern than our own. Cultural historians describe the Renaissance as operating with a 'one-sex' notion of sexual difference that goes back to the Greeks: where men and women are physiologically the same, but separated along a spectrum of difference, the male being seen as a later, more perfect version of the female. Thus, in anatomical illustrations from the period, what look like male sexual organs turn out to be female, the male form being seen as an inverted form of the female – literally turned inside out. This is in contrast to our modern, biologically determined version of sexual difference, where male and female are essentially, necessarily differentiated. Where we see an essential difference, early moderns saw things as nearly or almost the same.

Montaigne touches on these ideas in his essay 'Of a Monstrous Child', in which he relates how he saw a child that was being exhibited for money:

> Two days ago I saw a child that two men and a nurse . . . were carrying round to get a few sous by showing its strangeness . . . Underneath the breast it was joined to another child without a head . . . [and] one arm shorter than the other, which had been broken by accident at their birth. They were joined together face to face, as if a smaller child sought to throw its arms about the neck of a bigger one . . . The nurse told us that it urinated at both bodies, and that the members of the other were nourished, sensible, and in the same state as its own, excepting that they were shorter and thinner.

And then, in a subsequent edition, he adds to it another example of the variability of generation:

> I have just seen a shepherd in the Médoc, of about thirty years of age, who shows no sign of sexual organs: he has three holes where he makes water incessantly; he is bearded, has desire, and seeks contact with women.

Montaigne's choice of words – the child being shown for money (*montrer*); the shepherd who does not show (*montre*) any genitals – forges a link to the root of the word 'monster', from the Latin *monstrum*, meaning a show, a portent, a warning of God's providence. What Montaigne seems to be saying is that, whilst we see the child as something 'monstrous', to the shepherd 'showing' the male sexual organs might appear equally so. And maybe the shepherd's hermaphrodite attributes might be an integral version of something more entire: perhaps the culmination of the weaker child's attempt to embrace its sibling.

In his final handwritten additions to the essay, Montaigne goes on to ask whether 'That which we call monsters, are not so to God, who sees in the immensity of His work an infinity of forms. Who is to say that this figure that astonishes does not have a similarity to some other figure unknown to us' – perhaps to God him – *or her* – self?

And in the context of the varieties of sexual experience, Montaigne opens his mind to the possibility of a greater number of sexual-social norms. He speaks of countries where there are male brothels, and where marriage is contracted between men. In Rome he learns of a Portuguese sect that practises same-sex marriage 'with the same ceremonies . . . the same marriage service . . . and went to bed and lived together'. He speaks of countries where women accompany their men to war, and share in the fighting as well as the command.

And whilst in his offhand comments Montaigne seems very much a man of his time – he says for three beautiful women you must kiss fifty ugly ones, and quotes the Duke of Brittany on the fact that all a woman needed to know was the difference between her husband's doublet and his shirt – in the body of his essays Montaigne nonetheless tries, as much as he is able, to think outside the box, and to imagine what women think of men. And here, especially in his later additions, he puts men under the microscope, suggesting,

> In any case, inconstancy is perhaps rather more pardonable in them than in us. They may allege, as we do, the inclination to variety and novelty common to all of us; and secondly they may say, as we cannot, that they buy a cat in a bag.

Or, as we might say, a pig in a poke: women don't know how the man will perform when they get home, a situation Montaigne sees as exacerbated by the contemporary fashion for codpieces, which make an unrealistic 'show of the shape of our pieces under our Gascon hose'.

Left to their own devices, women are quite capable of managing on their own, as Montaigne finds during a visit to the nuns of Poussay, a foundation established for the education of girls. There is no requirement of virginity, except for the abbess and the prioress, and they all dress as they please, except for a little white veil. They freely receive people in their rooms, even to solicit them in marriage. Yet the greater number of them choose to spend the rest of their days there. Perhaps with such examples in mind (and Montaigne's niece Jeanne de Lestonnac was to go on to found a similar order for the education of young women), Montaigne concludes: 'Women are not at all in the wrong when they reject the rules of life that have been introduced into the world, inasmuch as it is the men who have made them without consulting them.'

But perhaps the most significant testament to Montaigne's attitude towards women can be seen in his relationship with

Marie de Gournay, who was to become Montaigne's editor and literary executor after his death. Born in 1565, she was thirty-two years younger than Montaigne, whom she had read in her late teens. They met after she had learned he was visiting Paris in 1588 and wrote to him, declaring 'the esteem she felt for his person and his book'. He responded by travelling to Picardy, to pay a visit to his admirer and her mother.

Montaigne gave de Gournay the title *'fille d'alliance'*, meaning adoptive daughter, which may sound a little strange, but her father had died when she was twelve, and Montaigne, with a wife and daughter of his own, may well have wanted to establish the relationship on a respectable footing. It is said he spent three months in her company: she transcribing some of his additions to the essays; he impressed by her humanistic learning. Clearly she was an impressive woman, with intellectual abilities beyond her age and well beyond her supposed station in life. And Montaigne's tribute to her talents was published in the posthumously printed 1595 edition of the *Essays*:

> I have taken pleasure to declare in several places the hopes I have of Marie de Gournay le Jars, my *fille d'alliance*, who is loved by me with a more than paternal love and included in my solitude and retirement as one of the better parts of my own being. There is nothing I regard more in the world than her. If youth is any indication, her soul will be one day capable of great things, among others the perfection of that holy friendship to which, we read, her sex has so far been unable to aspire . . .

As the passage was included only in the edition of the *Essays* that de Gournay herself edited, scholars have speculated, inconclusively, about the genuineness of this praise. As to the existence of an even closer relationship between Montaigne and de Gournay we will never know. But one passage in the *Essays* does suggest a more passionate attachment, certainly on her part:

> When I came from that famous assembly of the Estates at Blois, I had a little before seen a girl in Picardy, to attest to the ardour of her promises and her constancy, stab herself with the bodkin she wore in her hair, four or five lusty stabs in the arm, puncturing the skin and making herself bleed in good earnest.

However, given his inclusion of the description of her passionate self-harming in his text we cannot be sure whether such a display of violent constancy would have endeared her to Montaigne, or would have had the opposite effect.

❧

Montaigne ends 'On Some Verses of Virgil' with an intriguing metaphor:

> To conclude this notable commentary, which has escaped from me in a flow of chatter, a flow sometimes impetuous and hurtful.

Here picturing himself as almost feminine, writing the essay in something like a menstrual flow. And one wonders about those moments when Montaigne sees himself as labouring in expectation of giving birth to a kidney stone, or bathing in the women's bath at Lucca, or receiving one of Captain Paulino's gently administered enemas. He quotes Horace on a beautiful boy, indistinguishable from a line of girls 'with his long hair and ambiguous face', and himself mistakes a girl for a boy in a Church in Rome, asking her: 'Do you speak Latin?' He quotes Ovid on Tiresias, to whom 'Venus in both aspects was known', and he himself says that Cupid should be granted his fickle freedom, and is not served best when gripped in 'hairy, hoary hands'.

But whatever Montaigne's eventual sexuality, his final message is a challenge to the Stoic apartheid between men and women – 'I say that male and female are cast in the same mould: education and usage excepted, the difference is not great' – and to remind ourselves that it is our nearness, as well as our distance from our bodies, that makes us what we are. A familiar enough thought today, but one that taken in the context of sixteenth-century morality represents a shift of almost Copernican proportions: here, Montaigne returning our sexual instincts to the centre of the human orbit, the axis around which all our other practices turn. Unlike other forms of interaction, sex is based on 'reciprocity and mutual exchange'; it 'can only be paid in the same coin'. By contrast he castigates the hypocrisy and cruelty of what passes for conventional virtue, his indignation captured in the fervent additions he makes to his text:

> Everyone runs from seeing a man born, everyone queues to see him die. *To destroy him they search for a spacious field in clear daylight; to create him they creep into a dark and narrow ditch.* It is a duty to hide *and to blush* in making him, but it is glorious and the seed of many virtues in to unmake him.

Montaigne finally adds the bitter comment: '*We regard our being as a vice.*'

In opposition to this callous prudishness, Montaigne accepts the natural and inevitable attraction of the sexes, our deep desire for each other, and the centrality of sex in the natural landscape of our being: 'The whole movement of the world leads towards and resolves itself in this coupling; it is a matter infused throughout, it is the centre to which all things look.' In a German church he sees the men and women seated on the right and left of the central aisle: the church in its very structure affirming the lesson of the Fall. But later he witnesses the overcoming of such divisions in the timeless reconciliations of a village dance:

> After a short pause the gentleman goes to retrieve his partner, he kisses his hand to her; the lady receives the gentleman but does not kiss her own; and then putting

his hand under her armpit he embraces her, so that they are cheek to cheek . . .

The men are 'bare-headed and not very richly dressed', notes Montaigne, an indication of their modest status, but perhaps also – like his reflections on the nakedness of the inhabitants of the New World – a sign of their innocence and openness to each other, as the women place their hands on the shoulders of their partners, and they begin.

10

The Touch of a Familiar Hand

I looked upon death indifferently when I looked at it universally – as the end of life. I dismiss it in general, but in detail it worries me. The tears of a servant, the disposing of my clothes, the touch of a familiar hand, an ordinary phrase of comfort distresses me and reduces me to tears.

During the late 1580s Montaigne continued to play an active role in political and diplomatic life. In February 1588 he attended the court of Henry III on a mission from Henri de Navarre, an event noted by the English ambassador, Sir Edward Stafford, as the arrival of 'one Montigny, a very wise gentleman of the King of Navarre, whom he hath given his word to present unto the King'; adding in a later letter: 'The man is a Catholic, a very sufficient man; was once Mayor of Bordeaux, and one that would not take a charge to bring anything to the King that should not please him.' And a few days later the Spanish Ambassador Mendoza wrote to Philip II of the arrival of Montaigne, 'considered a man of understanding' – albeit adding rather rudely about our hero: 'though somewhat addle-pated'. Despite Mendoza's dismissal, however, it was soon after that Montaigne was briefly imprisoned in the Bastille by the Catholic League, in reprisal for the seizing of a Leaguist at Rouen. Clearly Montaigne was still considered a man of influence, and he was released only at the personal insistence of Catherine de' Medici.

Montaigne's continued engagement with the dangerous world of diplomacy, despite his avowed retirement, is matched in the essays by their preoccupation with the way people act on, influence, and affect each other through their physical being. Of course, in a world without email or telephones this is, to a large extent, unremarkable. Even so, Montaigne's diplomatic undertakings stress the significance of personal relations – and personal presence – in sixteenth-century politics, as Mendoza goes on to clarify in his letter, saying how Montaigne will himself influence the Countess of Navarre, and through her gain influence over Henri.

Montaigne's interest in these matters can be dated back to his earliest essays, where he writes about 'Of Quick or Slow Speech' and 'Ceremony at the Interview of Kings'. And indeed his very first essay – 'By Diverse Means We Arrive at the Same End' – opens by addressing the effect our behaviour has on others, and whether it possesses any reason or rationale:

> The most common way of softening the hearts of such as we have offended, when they are in possession of the power of revenge and hold us at their mercy, is by submission to move them to commiseration and pity. And yet, audacity and resolution, quite contrary means, have sometimes had the same effect.

He goes on to add that he possesses what would be seen as a 'cowardly' disposition towards compassion, as opposed to the rulings of the Stoics, who would have us consider pity 'a vice'. Yet the essay ends despondently, in line with the harshness of the times, cataloguing the gratuitous cruelty of Alexander in his treatment of Betis, the defiant leader of the Gazeans, whom he had dragged behind a cart until he was dead.

But whilst Montaigne's essays perhaps start off despairing of human relations, in a world torn apart by the violence of civil war, as they progress, particularly in the third volume of essays that he adds to his work in 1588, he reveals a growing interest in the physical dimension of human relations, writing on themes such as 'Of Three Kinds of Association', 'Of Physiognomy', and 'Of the Art of Conversation'. And in the manuscript additions that he makes to his text in the years up to his death, this interest seems to deepen. Despite the Stoics' view that we should see friends and relations as earthenware pots, and their deaths regretted little more than a breakage, Montaigne declares that the presence of grief is something for which we can never adequately prepare:

> No wisdom is so highly formed as to be able to conceive a cause of grief so vivid and so complete that it will not be increased by the actual presence, when the eyes and ears have a share in it . . .

He relates how he transported the body of his friend Monsieur de Grammont from the siege of La Fère and how in every place they passed onlookers responded with 'tears and lamentations by the mere solemn presence of our convoy, for even the name of the dead man was not known to them'.

No matter how stoically we distance ourselves from our emotions, we can never cut ourselves off entirely from the affective influence of others: 'the tears of a servant . . . the touch of a familiar hand', bring us back to ourselves and bind us to life once more.

Of course, much of Montaigne's awareness of the effect of our behaviour on others was gained through his experience as local lord, magistrate, and mayor, and as a negotiator during the civil wars. And the essays contain many reflections on the art of diplomacy. He says that most people make themselves appear as close to one's own position as they can, whereas he uses a style all his own:

> I say nothing to one man that I could not, at the right time, say to another, given a little alteration in the accent . . . There is no useful point whatsoever for which I would permit myself to tell them a lie. What has been entrusted to my silence, I conceal religiously; but I take as few things for concealing as I can. The secrets of princes are a troublesome charge to such as have no business with them.

He boasts that 'few men have negotiated between rival parties with less suspicion' and renounces duplicity in favour of candour: 'An open speech opens up another's speech and draws it out, like wine and love.' And in an essay, 'Of Anger', he describes his own strategy in tense negotiations, asking his opponent to let him vent his anger, as he will let them vent theirs, saying that the storm is produced only when they are not allowed to run their course – 'a useful rule,' he adds, 'but hard to observe'. Anger, he continues, can also be a useful weapon: he uses it 'for the better governing of my house', and confesses to being at times 'hasty and violent'. But it is also an unpredictable one: 'For we move other weapons, and this one moves us; our hand does not guide it, it guides our hand; it holds us, we do not hold it.'

On the other hand, a mild and accommodating demeanour can have an equally disastrous effect. He records the fate of Monsieur de Monneins, the governor of Bordeaux, who went out to quell a large mob during the Salt Tax riots of 1548, but conducted himself with a meek rather than a commanding mien, and hence was 'miserably slain'. By contrast he relates Socrates' composure whilst escaping from battle, noting 'the firmness and steadiness of his gaze . . . looking at friends and enemies, in a way to encourage the former and to show to the others that he was bound to sell his blood very dear'. And Montaigne himself relates how, when he was forced to flee during his country's disturbances, it 'served me in good stead' to do so in a way that did not appear 'bewildered or distraught', even though in reality he was 'not without fear'.

And whilst Montaigne seems in many ways a typical humanist, his writing reveals a desire to get beyond the page, and meet with the ancients face-to-face. He says he would rather see what Brutus did in 'his study and in his chamber than in the public square and the senate', and imagines sitting next to Alexander at table, seeing him talking and drinking and 'fingering his chess-men'. And he notes the ancients' own awareness of the physicality of others: how the Romans would caress the hands of great men on meeting, and kiss the cheeks of friends, like the Venetians of his own time. Hippomachus claimed to be able to tell a good wrestler simply by the way he walked. Caesar, he notes, scratched his head, a sign that he was preoccupied, whilst Alexander inclined his, slightly affectedly, a little to one side. Cicero wrinkled up his nose, which suggests a man given to scoffing. And Emperor Constantius, appropriately named,

> in public always looked straight ahead, without turning or flexing one way or the other . . . planting his body immovably, without allowing it to be moved by the motion of his coach, not daring so much as to spit, blow his nose, or wipe his face in front of the people.

This Montaigne notes in an essay 'Of Presumption', to show that even when we think we don't reveal things about ourselves, we reveal them all the same.

And Montaigne's alertness to people's physicality also takes in the parts of the body, the individual instruments in the overtures we make to others. He examines the bust of Titus Livius in Padua, his 'lean face suggesting a studious and melancholy man', and displays his knowledge of palmistry – how when a line cuts across the base of the forefinger it is a sign of a cruel nature. He even writes an essay 'Of Thumbs', relating how barbarian kings sealed treaties by clasping hands with their thumbs interlocked, then pricking them to suck each other's blood. He reminds us that in the Roman forum a 'thumbs down' meant a thumbs up and a 'thumbs up' meant a thumbs down. Spartan schoolmasters, he notes, would punish their pupils by biting them on their thumbs. And he quotes Martial on the evolutionary advantages (or disadvantage) offered by the opposable digit:

> Neither with the persuasion of charming words,
> Nor with the thumb's soft coaxing does it surge.

– i.e. masturbation.

And behind his interest in bodily behaviour, there perhaps lurks an anxiety in Montaigne about his own lack of physical presence. He says he is 'below middle height', only to raise himself up in his second edition to '*a little* below middle height'. This is part of the reason for his preference to go on horseback: 'On foot I get muddy up to my buttocks, and in our narrow streets small men tend to get jostled and elbowed for want of presence.' On his travels he says the best view of the prostitutes in Rome 'is from horseback; but that is a matter for poor creatures like me'. And at the end of the 'Apology' he makes a philosophical point that seems to be marked by his own personal experience, saying that there is no point trying to make 'the handful bigger than the hand, the armful bigger than an arm, and to hope to straddle higher than our legs'.

And perhaps this lack of stature is part of the reason for Montaigne's self-consciousness about himself: 'A certain carriage of the body and certain gestures betokening some vain and foolish pride.' He continues to carry 'a stick or staff in my hand even aiming at a kind of elegance in it and resting on it with an air of affectation'. And in social situations, even among his own men, Montaigne feels the pressure to make his presence felt before it evaporates:

> It is a great annoyance to be addressed, as you stand among your servants, with the question: 'Where is Monsieur?' and to receive only the remainder of the greeting that is made to your barber or your secretary. As it happened to poor Philopoemen: having been the first of his company to arrive at an inn where he was expected, his hostess, who did not know him and having seen that he was of an unsightly appearance, employed him to go and help her maids draw up water and make a fire for Philopoemen's arrival. The gentlemen in his service, arriving and surprising him as he was busied in this fine labour, asked him what he was doing. 'I am', he replied, 'paying the penalty for my ugliness.'

In the *Travel Journal*, Montaigne's secretary hints at his master's short stature during a visit to the tomb of Ogier the Dane near Paris, whose upper arm bone is as long as 'the length of the whole arm of a man of nowadays, of ordinary measure, and somewhat longer than Monsieur de Montaigne's' (which puts him somewhat shorter than the average height of around five feet and seven inches). Caius Marius, notes Montaigne, did not enlist any soldiers who were under six feet; and according to Aristotle, 'Little men are pretty but not handsome.' Whereas women are afforded all kinds of beauty, Montaigne complains, stature is the only beauty allowed in a man, despite the additional qualifications he adds to the second edition of his text (in italics):

> Where there is smallness, neither the breadth *and roundness* of the forehead, nor the brightness *and softness* of the eyes, nor the moderate shape of the nose, nor the littleness of the ears and mouth, nor the regularity and whiteness of the teeth, nor the uniform thickness of the beard, brown like the shell of a chestnut, *nor curly hair*, nor a well-rounded head, nor a fresh complexion, nor an agreeable expression of face, *nor a body without smell*, nor the regular proportion of the limbs, can make a handsome man.

He is, however, 'strong and well-knit'; 'my face full without being fat', and he goes around with 'my face and my heart open', his voice 'loud and emphatic', and 'my head erect'. He says that 'movement and action put life into words' especially with those like himself, who 'move briskly and become heated'. He is quick to remove his hat: 'especially in summer, and never receive a salutation without returning it, whatever the status of the man may be, unless he is in my service'.

Between the lines of Montaigne's writing, increasing as it

evolves through his *Travel Journal*, the various editions of his essays, and his relationship with his cat, is an intuitive sense of the disciplines we would now call proxemics – the anthropology of people's relationship to each other in space – and also kinesics – what their movements and gestures reveal. At the heart of these studies is the idea that the physical distance between people is intrinsically linked to their social and emotional intimacy. It is from here that we derive such terms as 'personal space' (anywhere between 1½ and 4 feet), and 'intimate space' (anywhere closer). As the founder of proxemics, Edward T. Hall, wrote in the sixties: 'Like gravity, the influence of two bodies on each other is inversely proportional not only to the square of their distance but possibly even the cube of the distance between them.' Or, as Walt Whitman said more poetically: 'Every cubic inch of space is a miracle.'

This proxemic sense is a faculty we have largely lost or become unconscious of since the Renaissance. But it is an awareness that was second nature to people of Montaigne's time, what might almost be called the sixteenth century's sixth sense. Art historians thus speak of the art of 'body-arranging' in Renaissance art, where the distribution of bodies in space does not equate to a naturalistic depiction, but frequently articulates dynastic and diplomatic links. Dance represented a way of codifying these affiliations, used by the court as not simply entertainment but a way of giving tangible form to the intimacies and alliances between rulers and their nobility. And clearly Montaigne's awareness of such things is linked to his aristocratic status, where his relationships to his fellow noblemen and the King were conducted through affiliations of clientage and personal acquaintance. Montaigne's boast that Henri de Navarre slept in his bed when he visited his house might strike us as a slightly embarrassing assertion, but for Montaigne there could be no clearer expression of the closeness of their *amitié*.

Montaigne thus observes how not only every country, but every city and profession 'has its own forms of civility', and describes how manners 'smooth over the first approaches to sociability and friendliness'. From his retirement he keeps making 'sidelong glances' at the attractions of power: 'A nod, a friendly word from a great man, a gracious look, tempt me.' And in his essay 'Of the Education of Children' he says he would have the child's 'outward manners, and his social behaviour, *and the carriage of his person*, formed at the same time as his mind'. He says that we wish to know our neighbours, not only in terms of their kinship and alliances, but 'to have them as friends and build a relationship and understanding with them'. And he remembers the advice his father gave him: 'to consider the man who stretches out his arms to me rather than the one who turns his back upon me', meaning the people and the peasants of his region.

He knows that loans asked for in person are more difficult to refuse than those requested by letter, and he says he understands others 'by their silence and their smiles, and perhaps understand them better at the dining-table than in the council-chamber'. Facile and vacuous speeches are redeemed by the 'gravity, the gown, and the fortune of him that speaks'. Philosophers, similarly, are no less affected by the power of others' presence. He quotes Socrates on the electric charge felt at the graze of a beloved's arm:

> With my shoulder touching his shoulder, and my head close to his, as we were reading together in a book, I

suddenly felt a pricking in the shoulder, if you will believe me, like the bite of an insect; and for more than five days it tingled, and a continual itching crept into my heart.

'What!' exclaims Montaigne, 'Socrates! – of all souls the most chastened, and at the mere touch of a shoulder!' But why not, he adds: 'Socrates was a man, and didn't want to be or be seen as anything else.'

And Montaigne goes on to speak of knowledge, not in purely abstract terms, but as a form of meeting. He says his brain is slow and muddied, 'but what it once grasps it . . . embraces very closely', and describes 'grasping the forms, the features, the bearing and the face of truth'. He says that places and books revisited 'smile at me with a fresh novelty'. And he quotes Socrates' comparison of himself to a midwife, assisting others in their intellectual labour:

opening their organs, anointing their channels, facilitating their birth, passing judgement on the child, baptizing it, nursing it, strengthening it, swathing and circumcising it, exercising and employing his skill in the perils and fortunes of others.

The Greek philosopher Zeno similarly saw the hand as embodying thinking, and communicated,

by gestures his conception of the division of the faculties of the mind: the hand spread out and open signified appearance; the hand half shut and the fingers slightly bent, consent; the fist closed, comprehension; when with the left hand he closed that fist more tightly, knowledge.

The best minds, Montaigne says, 'are those which are far-reaching, open and ready to embrace everything'.

And adding to the 'Apology for Raymond Sebond' in the years up to his death, Montaigne puts his finger on what it is that he wishes to defend about Sebond's conception of faith:

> The divine majesty has thus to some extent allowed itself to be circumscribed in corporeal limits for our own benefits. His supernatural and celestial sacraments have the signs of our earthly condition; his worship is expressed by means of rituals and words aimed at the senses; for it is man that believes and prays . . . it would be difficult to make me believe that the sight of our crucifixes and the paintings of that piteous agony, the ornaments and ceremonious movements of our churches, that the voices attuned to the devotion of our thoughts, and all that passion of the senses did not warm the souls of the people with a religious emotion of very beneficial effect.

One wonders whether Montaigne's rather complex conception of religion doesn't amount to seeing it as something like an extension of our proxemic senses, akin to the sociological idea of religion as 'the extension of social relations beyond the social'. For Montaigne, objects and locations thus gain an almost sacramental function, as stepping-stones to a long-lost physical propinquity. In the Vatican library he admires an ancient Greek Acts of the Apostles, the massive gold letters so lavishly applied 'that as you pass your hand over it you can feel the thickness . . . a kind of writing we have since lost'. Caesar's gown excited Rome almost as much as his actual presence, and even buildings and locations have the capacity to move us:

> Is it by nature or by an error of the fancy that the sight of places, which we know have been haunted and inhabited

by persons of whom the memory is esteemed, moves us, more than to hear a recital of their acts or to read their writings? . . . I like to think of their faces, their bearing, and their clothing. I ruminate on those great names between my teeth, and make them resound in my ears . . . I wish I could see them talk, walk and sup!

And of his own dead, he says, more movingly:

How satisfying it would be to hear somebody describe the manners, *the face, the countenance, the common words*, and the fortunes of my ancestors. How attentively I would listen! Truly, it would be the sign of an evil nature to despise so much as the pictures of our friends and predecessors, *the fashion of their clothes and of their arms. I preserve the handwriting, the seal, the breviary, and a particular sword which they used, and I have not banished from my study some long sticks which my father normally carried in his hand.*

The memory 'of a farewell, an action, a particular charm' is affecting to us, as is the mere sound of a name 'as it rings in our ears: "My poor master!", or "My great friend!", "Alas, my dear father!", or "My sweet daughter!"'.

Montaigne's awareness of others' bodies is thus very different from our modern Western, post-Cartesian perspective, where we see selves as distinct from and more important than the bodies in which they are housed. The clearest echoes of Montaigne's view thus comes from outside the Western tradition, in the work of the twentieth-century Japanese philosopher Watsuji Tetsurō . Watsuji describes the nature of the self using the notion of 'betweenness' (*aidagara*): our instinctive sense of our relation to other bodies in space. This language of 'betweenness' might seem rather touchy-feely, but we only have to look around our homes and workplaces to see how intrinsic it is to our sense of everyday life – how we are instinctively aware of the difference between public and private spaces, how we reserve our personal space for lovers and family, and how transgressions of these borders are felt in a way of which we cannot help but be aware. And it is this 'betweenness', according to Watsuji, that provides the ineluctable gravity to human relations, like that of the magnetic 'pull' that draws a mother back to her unattended child. But as well as mother and child, husband and wife, it is also felt between friends:

> To feel like seeing a friend is to tend to go physically near them . . . It is therefore clearly a mistake to regard this relationship as a psychological relationship without the interconnection between physical bodies. However its psychological moment may be contained, the physical bodies still draw themselves to each other and are interconnected. It is neither simply a physical relationship nor a psychological nor the simple conjunction of the two.

And here, of course, one is reminded of La Boétie's final plea: 'do you refuse me a place'? For no matter what we might *think* about friendship – in terms of its spiritual or philosophical meaning – its basic manifestation is in a desire for physical proximity – a sense of *betweenness*. Friends, to put it simply, are people that you go and see. Despite the discourse of stoical humanism, it is a relationship founded on presence, not by absence.

At the most basic level, therefore, Holbein's *Ambassadors* (p. 34) is a painting about friendship as it shows two men standing next to each other. And if we look again at Montaigne's letter describing La Boétie's death (p. 32), we see that its other-worldly pose is continually undercut by his awareness of his friend's physical being, a consciousness of the movements and gestures of his friend. He is due to dine with him, then urges La Boétie to leave Bordeaux but not to travel too far. He visits him, goes away, and then returns and remains constantly at his side. He takes his pulse and then, in an attempt to reassure him, asks him to take his. He rather selfishly emphasizes his own closeness compared to La Boétie's wife, who stays for most of the time in an adjoining room. And he finally records La Boétie's call to him, 'My brother . . . stay close to me,' followed by his delirious ramblings about being denied 'a place' – a final moving reminder that we cannot help but see life as the experience of being near to other people, and death as a last dislocation, the final seat-stealing in a game of irredeemable musical chairs.

And when Montaigne returns to La Boétie in his essay 'Of Friendship', written ten years after his death, he recalls, not simply the philosophical bond between them, nor the nature of La Boétie's character, but more specifically the moment of their first meeting, where they found each other, and became: 'so bound together, that from that moment on nothing could be as close as we were to one another'.

In this sense the special nature of friendship is not to do with the fact that it comes with no obligations, but because friendship necessarily activates and invigorates our proxemic senses: it arises when two bodies that had once been unknown to each other meet; as Montaigne says: they 'embraced' each other 'by our names', seeking each other out amidst the throng of a civic feast. Montaigne's writing about friendship thus shows a man profoundly impressed by the stoical composure of his dead friend, yet also drawn to friendship as constituted by physical proximity, an unspoken, invisible but nourishing force.

❧

What makes Montaigne's proxemic awareness all the more pressing, however, is that he sees it as a sense that is being progressively anaesthetized by the political and religious violence of his time – 'not a change in the entire mass, but its dissipation and rending asunder'. In wartime identities become obscured; friends might possibly be foes. But the other person's body can also become a thing of hatred rather than knowledge; an object of a perverted, voyeuristic desire. Montaigne speaks of people murdering for the sake of murdering, hacking off men's limbs and thinking of new forms of torture 'for no other end but to enjoy the delightful spectacle of the piteous gestures and motions'. He speaks of how 'the common rabble become inured to war and show their bravery by staining themselves up to the elbows in blood and by ripping up bodies that lie prostrate at their feet'. In civil war these cruelties attain an almost inverted sacramental function in what the historian Natalie Zemon-Davies describes as 'rites of violence', where the annulling of people's empathetic, proxemic awareness is effected by the ritual mutilation of the other, where one's enemies are rendered *unrecognizable*, and one's sense of guilt becomes anaesthetized and dulled.

During the height of the violence Montaigne thus writes of how:

some countrymen came to inform me in great haste that they had just left, in a wood that belongs to me, a man injured with a hundred wounds, still breathing, who asked them for pity's sake to give him water and help him up. They said they did not dare to go near him, and ran off for fear the officers of justice might catch them there . . .

Such callousness, moreover, is exacerbated by the cold Stoicism of the age, where pity or sympathy is seen as weakness, and where even the closest relationships are estranged and cut off – as the ruthless Royalist general Marshal de Monluc confesses to Montaigne following the death of his son, rebuking himself for his habitual 'paternal gravity and stiffness':

'And that poor boy,' he said, 'never saw in me anything other than a scowling and disdainful countenance, and took away with him a belief that I knew not how to love him or esteem him according to his deserts. For whom was I reserving the discovery of that singular affection I had for him in my soul? Was it not him that should have had all the pleasure of it and all the gratitude? I constrained and tortured myself to maintain this vain mask and thereby have lost the pleasure of his conversation, and of his affection along with it, for he could not be anything but cool towards me, having never received from me anything but harshness, nor experienced anything other than a tyrannical bearing.'

And adding to this sense of divisiveness is the increasing economic sophistication of sixteenth-century life. Montaigne writes an essay on how 'One Man's Profit is another Man's

Loss' and recalls a period when, as a result of the success of his estate, he hoarded his money, a process which seemed, however, to bring about only a sense of his own isolation:

> I made it a secret, and I, who dare talk so openly of myself, never spoke of my money but falsely, as do others, who being rich, pretend to be poor, and being poor, pretend to be rich, dispensing their consciences from ever saying sincerely what they have: a ridiculous and shameful prudence.

As a result he found himself plagued with anxieties, doubts, suspicions – 'moreover, incommunicable ones!'

Montaigne's sense of this divisiveness, and the growing alienation of sixteenth-century life, is encapsulated in his essay 'Of Coaches', which he adds to the *Essays* in 1588. Here he gives vent to his dislike of coaches, which firstly make him travel-sick, but also for the way coaches represent a separation from others, economically and proxemically, and hence epitomize the individualistic, acquisitive estrangement of his age – an age ruled by 'treason, luxury, avarice', where people are supplanted by things. And this he sees exemplified in the sacking of the New World, where 'under colour of friendship and good faith' millions were 'put to the edge of the sword . . . for the traffic in pearls and in pepper!'

Against this avaricious duplicity, he contrasts what he sees as the greatest feat of any civilization to date:

> the highway to be seen in Peru, built by the kings of the country, from the city of Quito as far as Cuzco (a distance of three hundred leagues), straight, even, twenty-five paces wide, paved . . . Where they came across mountains and rocks they carved through and levelled them, and

filled in the holes with stone and chalk. At the end of each stretch are beautiful palaces, furnished with provisions, clothing and arms, all for the benefit of travellers . . .

In contrast to the conquistadors' treachery, the road literally connects people, welcoming strangers with food and clothing. And this is emphasized by the fact that it was built not only by the collaboration of two kings, but also by a common effort on the part of the people, from stones that were ten feet square, using earthen ramps instead of scaffolding, and 'no other means of transport than the strength of their arms' – a joint bodily effort that symbolizes the physical cohesion of the people themselves. However, this is tragically ineffective against the Spaniards' superior technology, as Montaigne signals, getting back to his main topic:

> Let us return to our coaches. Instead of these, or any other vehicle, [the Peruvians] had themselves carried on the shoulders of men. That last King of Peru, on the day that he was taken, was thus carried on golden poles and seated in a golden chair in the midst of his army. As many of these chair-bearers as were slain . . . so many others emulated them, taking the place of the dead, in such a way that they could never cut him down, however great a slaughter they made of those people, until a horseman seized him by the body and dragged him to the ground.

The image of the toppled Atahualpa, his human cordon savagely slaughtered beneath him, himself dragged downward by the alien treachery of an individual horseman, seems to represent a sort of nadir for Montaigne.

What Europeans have lost, therefore, is their proxemic literacy: religious obstinacy, mercantilist materialism and our own self-love having obscured it from view. But Montaigne goes on to suggest that this is a literacy that can be relearned.

Hence the frequency and emotional appeal of motifs of meeting in Montaigne's writing: the Siamese twins in the essay 'A Monstrous Child', one seeking to embrace the other; and his description of the execution of the Egnatii by the triumvirs of Rome, who ran onto each other's swords and clasped 'each other with so tight an embrace that the executioners cut off both their heads at one stroke, leaving the bodies still linked'. He writes of how marriage is reinvigorated by 'the pleasure of meeting and parting at intervals', filling him with 'a fresh affection for my family and making the enjoyment of my house sweeter'. On his journey through Bavaria, Montaigne describes seeing a monument on the Brenner Pass, built to commemorate the meeting of Emperor Charles V and his brother in 1530 – 'seeking each other after having been eight years without seeing one another' – with a plaque showing them 'embracing each other'.

He likes bridges: he admires Basel's fine, wide wooden one over the Rhine and laments the fact that the new bridge in Paris (the Pont Neuf) would not be finished before his death (it was completed in 1604). And in his essay 'Of a Lack in Our Polity' he recalls his father's idea for a sort of labour exchange/lonely-hearts column, where a master might seek a servant, or 'company on a journey to Paris' or some suchlike thing. He regrets the deaths in poverty and neglect of the scholars Lilius Giraldus and Sebastien Castellio, when 'a thousand men would have welcomed them into their families . . . had they known'.

Montaigne's natural disposition is therefore naturally

gregarious: 'born for society and friendship'. He says pleasure has no flavour for him 'unless I can communicate it', and cites the view of the Greek philosopher Archytas, that heaven itself would be unbearable if experienced alone: 'to wander among those great and divine celestial bodies without a companion at one's side'.

And in his essays Montaigne uses the privilege of authorship to advertise for a companion, another La Boétie, to repeat his original meeting with his friend:

> Other than the benefit I draw from writing about myself, I hope for this other, that if there happens to be any worthy man who approves and is pleased by my humours before I die, he will try and meet with me . . .
>
> If I knew for sure of a man who was well-suited to me, truly, I would go a very long distance to find him. For we cannot, I think, pay too much for the sweetness of a sympathetic and agreement companion – Oh a friend!

– a call that was perhaps answered, although possibly not in the way he anticipated, in the devotion of Marie de Gournay.

But probably the best-known instance of Montaigne's interest in meeting and the power of proxemics comes in his essay 'Of the Art of Conversation'. Here speech serves as not simply a manifestation of thought, but an extension of the human body in which Montaigne celebrates the cut-and-thrust, the grappling and wrestling of joshing among friends. He says he disdains civility and art in his conversations, and prefers 'a strong and manly association and familiarity . . . like love that bites and scratches till the blood comes'. And in 'Of Experience' he elaborates on the fact that it is not what is being said, but how and why:

There is a voice for instructing, a voice for flattering, or to scold. I want my voice not only to reach him, but perhaps that it should hit him and pierce him. When I berate my lackey in a sharp and pointed tone, it would be fine of him to say: My master, speak more softly, I hear you well . . . A speech half belongs to him that speaks and half to him that hears. The latter must prepare to receive it according to the movement it takes. As with those who play tennis, the receiver moves around and takes up position according to the movements of the server and according to the stroke.

And linked to this is the idea that feelings and emotions are necessarily shared between ourselves. What Montaigne recognizes, 400 years before their discovery by scientists in 1996, is the existence of 'mirror neurons', or 'empathy neurons': neurons that fire when we watch another person performing an action or undergoing an experience. Moreover, this research suggests that verbal communication is built around this more ancient communicative system, based around the recognition of facial and physical gestures – i.e. that Montaigne's description of it as 'the true language of human nature' may not be far wrong. Montaigne thus says that he has an 'aping and imitative character'; 'whatever I contemplate, I adopt – a foolish expression, a disagreeable grimace, a ridiculous way of speaking'; 'I often usurp the sensations of another person'. Writing about sex, he confesses that 'the pleasure I give tickles my imagination more sweetly than that I feel', and yet says, equally, that the sight of another's pain 'materially pains me'. He speaks of the power of poetry to transmit emotion: the passion that inspires the poet 'also strikes a third person when he hears him discuss and recite it, like a magnet that not only attracts a needle, but also conveys into it the power to attract others'. And in the theatre, anger, sorrow, hatred, pass in a similar way through poet, actor and audience: like a chain of magnetized needles, 'suspended one from the other'. And this reminds us of Montaigne's talent as a boy actor, his 'great assurance of countenance and flexibility of voice and gesture in adapting myself to any part'.

And yet, such is the power of this imitative faculty that it can also work both ways:

> Simon Thomas was a great physician of his time. I remember that I met him one day at the house of a rich old consumptive, and whilst talking with his patient about the method of treatment, he told him that one way was to give him the pleasure of my company, and so that by fixing his eyes on the freshness of my face, and his thought on the overflowing liveliness and vigour of my youth, and filling all his senses with my flourishing youthfulness, his condition might be improved. But he forgot to say that at the same time mine might get worse.

Despite civil war and the divisiveness of his time, Montaigne thus sees human beings as still possessing a capacity for sympathy and reciprocity; we cannot help but see – and experience – the similarities and likenesses between others and ourselves, and our sense of life is intimately linked to this 'betweenness' between us. What obstructs our recognition of this fact, however, lies not simply within others, but within our own selves. At the heart of Montaigne's work is therefore an attempt to 'get away from the vulgar qualities that are within us . . . and recover possession of ourselves'. Here Montaigne attempts to reboot the self and clear out its cluttered memory; to reintroduce ourselves to ourselves and hence to our fellow man. But such a reconciliation is a much more difficult undertaking, something that is far more slippery and difficult to observe. How do you go about 'meeting' with yourself; how do you draw near? Montaigne's answer is to make use of a new ingredient, something far removed from traditional philosophy, something drawn from his estate and the land around him, something more home grown.

II

A Dog, a Horse, a Book, a Glass

Finding myself in this plight, I wondered by how many slight causes and objects my imagination nourished in me the regret of losing my life. Out of what atoms the weight and difficulty of this dislodging from life was built up in my soul; and how many frivolous thoughts we give room to in so great an affair. A dog, a horse, a book, a glass, and what not, counted for something in my loss.

In the final years of his life, Montaigne's suffering at the hands of his kidney stones increased. But whilst exiled to what seemed to be the margins of life, he considers the simple things that intrude upon our acceptance of dying. They seem trifling yet somehow command our attention, and in fact seem to grow in meaning the more inconsequential they are: 'A dog, a horse, a book, a glass . . .'

Montaigne was a seigneur, a member of the *noblesse d épée* and a provincial gentleman of letters. But he was also a *vigneron*, a winemaker. Looking out from his study he could see the frost pinching the vines, January's pruning and tying, the sun warming the grapes and the bustle of the September *vendange*. He could see the grapes being taken to the presses opposite his tower and the barrels loaded onto carts to be taken down to the river, and from there carried onwards on to the ports upriver and westwards into the sea. Barrels, bottles and glasses, drunkards, vineyards and vines totter and weave through the lines of his writing. He thinks about the flavour of wine in antiquity, the strange sobriety of drunken German soldiers, and the occult mysteries of fermentation. When he is travelling he feels free from day-to-day worries, but when he is at home he 'suffers like a winemaker'.

Winemaking in Montaigne's region dated back to the centuries after Caesar's conquest of Gaul. The fourth-century poet Ausonius describes seeing the Moselle, and being suddenly transported by its likeness to the area around his native Bordeaux: the 'hills bright green with vines, / and the pleasant stream below'. After the Black Death and the Hundred Years War, the economy declined, but during Montaigne's century it stabilized and began to put down fresh roots. The towns and villages were replenished as peasants poured in from the Massif Central; the soil was reawakened and revived.

And wine was central to this rejuvenation. Trade with England, Brittany and later the Dutch, and the growth of urban populations encouraged the planting of new vineyards upstream from Bordeaux, where city nobles and bourgeoisie like the Lestonnacs, Pontacs and Mullets began buying up land from the peasants with handfuls of American silver. And as they consolidated their estates – as Montaigne's family was so successful in doing – they turned to wine rather than wheat as their main product. Fields were amalgamated, smallholdings disappeared. The peasants increasingly found themselves working for the larger owners as sharecroppers, taking loans for food and clothing throughout the year then settling accounts with the fruits of their own labour.

Nearby, the Dordogne, the Lot and the Garonne provided the arteries for this recuperation, as shallow-hulled gabares nosed their way towards Libourne, Bordeaux and ports on the Gironde, the wine then loaded onto coasters and caravels for the long voyages north. In 1553 Montaigne's schoolmaster, George Buchanan, returned from an unhappy stay in Portugal and greeted France with a Latin eulogy which seems to have been sweetened by the natural and mercantile fertility surrounding Bordeaux:

> Hail, nurturing mother of the fine arts,
> Your healthy air and fruitful soils,
> Hills softly shaded in vines,
> Cattle-rich glades, well-watered valleys,
> Green meadows decorated with flowers,
> Meandering rivers carrying sails,
> Fish-filled ponds, streams, lakes, and sea,
> And west and south, shores full of harbours
> Receiving the world, and sharing with it,
> In turn, your riches without a hint of greed.

Figures for the region as a whole show it exporting an average of around 30,000 barrels of wine a year during the late sixteenth century. The Dutch being particularly keen on white wine, much of it grown upriver towards Montaigne and Bergerac. To customers in Amsterdam, Bruges, and London it offered an affordable, unpolluted alternative to water which could also ease the stresses and strains of city life.

In this picture, Montaigne might be considered as one of the older class of seigneurial owners, but he too turned from wheat to wine as his main crop: exploiting the chalk soils and natural drainage of the south-facing slopes of Montaigne; the vine roots drinking in potassium and nitrogen, phosphorus and magnesium, resulting in a drink, according to Colette, savouring of 'the taste of the earth'. And it is perhaps the potential in his estate that also helps to explain Montaigne's retirement from his job as a magistrate; he writes how he has 'continued to prosper beyond my expectations and calculations: I seem to get more out than I put in.'

A seventeenth-century woodcut entitled *Autumn* (pictured at the start of this chapter) gives a sense of Montaigne's world, where an ageing seigneur and his wife pause during the *vendange* or grape-picking to observe the fertile industry going on around them: the seigneur's paring knife indicating his links to the land and his people; the apples in his wife's skirt showing nature's bountiful largesse; and the cart in the background, weighed down with barrels, indicating a pension pot maturing nicely.

Montaigne cannot help but see his own life as similarly entwined with the natural and viticultural rhythms that surround him:

> It is one of the principal obligations that I have to my fortune, that the course of my bodily state has been conducted each according to its season: I have seen the leaf, the flower, and the fruit; and now I see the drying up . . .

Yet the world of the *vigneron* was more demanding than that of the wheat farmer, more technically difficult, requiring man-management and a firm hand on the wheel. Retirement for Montaigne thus was not necessarily as peaceful as he might originally have hoped. He complains about the poverty and fractiousness of the hundreds of people dependent on him, and quotes Horace on the winegrower's litany of woes:

> Either hail has spoiled your vines,
> Or the soils treachery; trees that
> Blame the rains, and the stars,
> and winter's iniquity.

He tells how 'when the vines freeze in my village, my priest declares that the wrath of God is upon the human race'. And concludes that Diogenes 'answered according to my humour' when he was asked what sort of wine he like best: 'Another man's.'

Of course Montaigne would not have necessarily been involved in the back-breaking work himself. A steward was employed to supervise the care of the vines: digging around and manuring them, pruning them so that the plant's energies flowed into the fruit. But as seigneur, Montaigne would have been responsible for calling the *ban de vendange*, the beginning of the grape harvest, a moment of great importance for the economic well-being of the community. Here large numbers of workers needed feeding and organizing. Vats and wine-presses needed to be inspected and repaired. And on top of this, Montaigne would have had the responsibility for marketing and selling his wine, through the new breed of official agents or *courtiers*, but inevitably through family contacts as well. As mayor he defended Bordeaux wines from foreign imports, introducing rules against them being put in the same casks. And Montaigne seems to have been experimenting with improving the quality of his product, showing an awareness of how wine 'changes its flavour in cellars, according to the changes and seasons of the vine from which it came' and recognizing the importance of the lees for keeping it alive. When travelling through Germany and Italy he begins to complain when the 'old' wine has run dry.

The language of wine and winemaking thus comes easily to Montaigne. Perhaps the first essay he composes, 'Of Idleness', opens with an image from Virgil, comparing his mind to light dancing on the ceiling, reflected off the water in a vat (a familiar sight to a winemaker), and goes on to express the hope that retirement might make his mind 'weightier and riper with time'. And when writing about the education of children, he very easily makes the transition to the training of his vines:

> Just as in agriculture the methods that precede the planting, and the planting itself, are certain and easy, but as soon as what is planted comes to life, there are a great variety of methods and difficulties in cultivating it. Similarly with humans: there is little industry in planting them; but as soon as they are born we are charged with diverse concerns, full of troubles and fears, in training and nourishing them.

He talks of turning to another subject in terms of trying a different vat (*cuvée*). And addressing his own melancholy, he tells how a docile spirit needs reinforcing: 'some good sound strokes of the mallet to force down and tighten the hoops of this cask which is getting loose and weak in the seams and going completely to bits'. He writes of the difficulty of extracting any 'juice and substance' from reading Cicero, and quotes Seneca on the pleasant melancholy of the memory of dead friends: 'like the bitter taste in wine when it is old'. And in words that Shakespeare was to echo in *Macbeth*, he likens the remainder of his life to the dregs of a barrel: 'I have come to the bottom of the cask, which is beginning to taste of the lees.'

In this language, however, Montaigne reflects the centrality of wine in early modern society, an everyday drink that was nevertheless blessed with a multiplicity of religious and therapeutic virtues. The country people around Montaigne thus 'make use of nothing, in all sorts of distempers, but the strongest wine they can get, mixed with a great deal of saffron and spice'. He knows from his own experience how 'there are some simples that moisten, and others that dry . . . that mutton nourishes me, and wine warms me'. He even admits to a moment of food-faddishness when he fed a goat only on white wine and herbs and then slaughtered it to see if the healing powers of its flesh were all they were reported to be. (He goes off the idea, when it emerges that the goat is suffering from stones itself.) But the class assumptions behind wine are also revealed here, with the more subtly flavoured white wine being seen as more suitably upper-class. On the other hand, the red-blooded warmth of red wine was seen as an indispensable part of the solder's armoury. Montaigne tells how French soldiers marching north to Luxembourg were so cold that that their wine rations froze; but they simply chopped it up with hatchets and carried it off in their helmets.

Wine is also seen as a common bond, something that people are assumed to understand and share despite their differences – a useful thing to present by way of greeting. On his travels he thus receives from the deaconess of Remiremont a barrel of wine along with some partridges and artichokes. Signor Ludovico Pintesi sends him twelve flagons of sweet wine and figs. In Constance the burgomasters deliver wine to Montaigne's inn, and in Augsburg fourteen large vessels of wine are presented to him by 'seven sergeants in livery and an eminent officer of the crown'.

But in its universality, wine also reveals national characteristics. The French avoid the bottom of the cask, whilst in Portugal the lees are fit for a prince. In Florence the locals add snow to their glasses to cool it (elsewhere wine was often warmed). In Germany they prefer quantity rather than quality and serve it in large pitchers, even inviting their servants to dip in. There the glasses are too big; in Italy too small. And when visiting Basel, people complain to Montaigne how dissolute and drunk everyone is. As for drinking bouts, Montaigne says that he 'was never invited to any except out of courtesy, and never attempted any'.

In the body of the *Essays* wine provides Montaigne with an umbilical link to the ancients, where Montaigne can sit down and drink with them man to man. He tells how the ancients took breaths as they drank and liked to cool wine with ice even in winter. And antiquity also had its own ranking and ratings – Montaigne quotes Homer on the sublimity of wine from Chios, whose townspeople were taught the art of winemaking by Oinopion, the son of Dionysus himself (according to Pliny, 121 BCE was a particularly good year).

Wine is therefore a constant ingredient in Montaigne's writing. But what is most revealing is when he comments on his own tastes in wine, his own likes and dislikes. Here Montaigne reflects the growth of a distinctly more modern, commercial market for wine, one devoted to providing not simply sustenance, but pleasure and taste. Traditionally winemaking expertise had been concentrated in monastic communities, but over the course of the Middle Ages there developed a wider culture of connoisseurship. In the *La Bataille des Vins*, by the thirteenth-century poet Jean d'Andeli, a priest samples seventy wines for the King, who wants to know which is the best. Before collapsing drunk, the priest excommunicates a number of acidic northern wines, as well as beer simply for being English. The prize eventually goes to a wine from Cyprus, with its reassuringly expensive, sweet strength. Unsurprisingly, the thirteenth-century troubadour Bertrand de Born complained that the nobility were getting

soft with all this talk of wine rather than warfare, Dante
suitably immortalizing him in *The Divine Comedy* holding not
a glass of Chablis, but his own severed head.

But among the new class of winemakers surrounding
Bordeaux in the sixteenth century the art of winemaking rose
to new heights. They researched new techniques – manuring
the rootstocks, planting in rows, maturing in barrels and
installing presses. For in this expanding and competitive
market taste was at a premium. Nobles and city merchants did
not want to drink the locals' watery *piquette* – made from the
remains of the already crushed grape. They wanted something
richer, finer, to complement the other symbols of nobility that
they actively pursued. And since labelling and branding were
not yet established, taste was the sole criterion determining
price – as growers, merchants and sailors and crowded around
the new barrels, drawing up samples in their *tastevins*.

Increasing trade served as an encouragement to this continuing sophistication. In 1562, the London merchant Henry Machyn recorded the celebrations surrounding the christening of William Harvey's daughter in the parish of St Bride's, noting – and the luxury of it seemed worth noting – the rich choice of wines on offer:

> and there was as great [a] banquet as I have [ever] seen, and wassail of hipocras [spiced wine], French wine, Gascoyne wine, and Rhenish [wine] with great plenty, and all their servandes had a banquet in the hall with divers dishes.

And in 1586 William Harrison described how contemporary consumers enjoyed an even wider choice:

> as claret, white, red, French, etc., which amount to about 56 sorts ... but also of the 30 kinds of Italian, Grecian, Spanish, Canarian etc. whereof vernage, cut, piment, raspis, muscatel, rumeny, bastard, tyre, osey, caprike, clary and malmsey ... so the stronger the wine is, the more it is desired.

Among other wines being imported were vintages from Alicante, Burgundy, Nantes, Oleron, and Rochelle, as well as newcomers from the eastern Mediterranean like Muscatel and Sack. In the light of such competition, the taste of a vintage could mean the difference between profit and loss. Guides were thus written to this revived science of winemaking, such as Henri Estienne's *Vinetum* of 1536. And in 1601 Nicolas-Abraham de La Framboisière advised:

> To judge the quality and the goodness of wine, it is necessary to carefully scrutinize the estate and constitution of each wine, and to taste every year, to give a confident opinion on it. Some years the wines of Burgundy take the

prize; in other years the wines of Orléans surpass; never are the wines of Anjou more excellent than any others; and most often the wines of Ay hold the first place in goodness and perfection.

In Cervantes's *Don Quixote*, this new sensitivity to taste is satirized when Sancho Panza boasts of being able to tell of a wine 'its country, its kind, its flavour and soundness, the changes it will undergo', simply from its smell, a talent he owed to one of his ancestors, who on smelling and tasting a wine described it as leathery with a touch of iron, only for the barrel to be upended to reveal a key with a leather fob.

Questions of quality and taste thus played an increasingly important role in the market for wine in the late sixteenth century. But it also seems likely Montaigne was blessed with a very sensitive palate himself, suggesting that he was what would be now called a 'supertaster', i.e. among that 25% of the population capable of tasting more intensely than anyone else, and able to detect flavours imperceptible to anyone else. Striking a Stoic note, he ostensibly distances himself from this sensitivity – 'We should take the whip to a young man who amused himself choosing between the taste of wines and sauces' – yet he goes on to say that in old age he is doing just that: 'At this moment I am learning it. I am much ashamed of it, but what should I do? I am still more ashamed and vexed at the circumstances that drive me towards it.'

Montaigne even coins the phrase 'science de gueule' (science of the gullet), telling how the cook of Cardinal Caraffa spoke of the art of gastronomy 'with gravity and a magisterial air', as if he were discoursing of 'the government of an empire'. And this was the beginning of the great age of French cookery, reaching its apogee in the seventeenth century when the famed chef Vatel committed suicide on eve of the King's feast when he realized he had run out of fish.

Montaigne's sense of taste is also accompanied with a very acute sense of smell (as we now know, our sense of taste is largely dependent upon the olfactory membrane in our noses). He writes an essay 'Of Smells', where he says how he likes 'very much to be surrounded with good smells, and I hate bad ones beyond measure, and detect them from further away than anyone else'. He describes his nose as a 'marvel' in how sensitive it is. He describes the sweetness of a healthy child's breath and how the whiff of his gloved hand will stay with him all day. His fondness for Venice and Paris is spoiled by the stink of their muddy marshes, and he prefers the stoves of Austria to the smoky fireplaces of home. The best smell for a man or a woman, he says, is to smell of nothing.

Montaigne's olfactory and gustatory sensitivity is especially apparent in his *Travel Journal*, which becomes a veritable sixteenth-century *Parker's Wine Buyer's Guide* as he sniffs and tastes, swills and expectorates the winemaking efforts of other regions. In Plombières both wine and bread are bad. In Schongau they only serve new wine, ordinarily very soon after it is made. In Augsburg 'the wines are good . . . and more often than not white', as are the wines of Sterzing. In Vicenza in November the old wines that they brought with them are already beginning to go off, so that:

> we regretted leaving those of Germany, although they were for the most part aromatic and have various scents which they find delicious, especially sage, which they call sage wine, which is not bad, when you get used to it, for otherwise their wine is good and generous.

The wines of Basel 'are so slight that our gentlemen found them even weaker than those of Gascony when these are well baptized [watered down]; and yet all the same they are very delicate'. In Florence he finds the wines 'undrinkable . . . for those who hate an insipid sweetness'. But at Bagni di Lucca a fellow bather, the Minister Friar of St Francis, sends him some 'very good wine' and some marzipan, and Montaigne observes how the local wine economy works:

> Every day one could see being brought to this place from all parts different samples of wines in little bottles, so that the visitors there who liked them might place an order. And yet there were very few good wines. The white wines were light but bitter and crude . . . unless you sent to Lucca or Pescia for the white Trebbiano, strong mature, though not too delicate for all that.

Later the Trebbiano, and its 'sweet, heady' taste gives him a migraine.

Montaigne also takes a professional interest in local winemaking techniques. In Massa di Carrara he is 'forced' to drink new wines, which, he notes, are clarified 'with a certain kind of wood and the whites of eggs'; they lack none of the colour of old wines, but have 'an indefinable, unnatural taste'. He noses around vineyards, noting the start of the harvest in Lucca, and how the cardinal at Urbino has grafted his vines. He sees the carved satyr in the vineyard of Cardinal Sforza and compares the vineyards of Rome with those of Bordeaux: 'which are gardens and pleasure spots of particular beauty, and where I saw how art can make use of a rugged, hilly and uneven spot; for here they derive charms that cannot be equalled in our level places'.

But perhaps the most important thing about Montaigne's relationship with wine is the way it enters his bloodstream, giving him a new way to think about the whole process of 'essaying', and ultimately to thinking about life itself. For what does Montaigne mean by '*essais*'? Most commentators translate it as 'trials', 'tests' or 'attempts', with the emphasis on a slightly humbled intellectual capacity, which would accord with our modern preoccupation with the sceptical element in Montaigne. But to Montaigne's contemporaries, '*essais*' could also mean simply 'tastes', or 'tastings'. If we look at the history of the word 'essay' or 'assay' (an early form which was also shared with English), it is thus very clearly linked to food and wine. A medieval English recipe for the spiced wine hipocras instructs the reader to add the ingredients and then 'take a pece, and assay it; and yet hit be enythyng to stronge of ginger, alay it with synamon'. The fifteenth-century French chronicler Olivier de La Marche writes extensively of the whole etiquette of the 'assay' of a Lord's wine in a noble household: how the cup-bearer 'carries his goblet to the prince, and puts some wine in his glass, then re-covers his goblet and makes his essay [*assay*]'. (Montaigne had in fact read La Marche's *Memoires* and very possibly gained the inspiration for his title from him.) And in his French–English dictionary of 1611 Randle Cotgrave thus defines the French *essay* as: a 'proofe, tryall, experiment; an offer, attempt; a tast, or touch of a thing to know it by; also the tast, or Essay taken of a Princes meat, or drinke' – a usage that is represented in George Herbert's 'The Agonie':

Who knows not Love, let him assay
And taste that juice, which on the crosse a pike
Did set again abroach; then let him say
If ever he did taste the like.
Love is that liquour sweet and most divine,
Which my God feels as bloud; but I as wine.

What is also interesting is that this process of essaying or assaying, or tasting – often to check that wine had not been adulterated – was also one of the responsibilities of the local lord. In 1559 the Earl of Pembroke's rights were said to include: 'the assise and assay of bread, wine, beer and other victuals; the scrutiny of weights and measures, and the amendment and correction of the same'. Taste had to be regularized in some way, and in the absence of objective standards of measurement the obvious way to do it was to follow the lines of political power and leave it to the discrimination of the local seigneur.

What seems to have happened is that, subsequent to (and obviously in great part because of) Montaigne, the word 'essay' has gained a much more rational, intellectual sense, and become synonymous with 'chapters' or short prose disquisitions. Montaigne, however, never referred to his chapters as 'essays', and initially entitled his book *Essais de Messire Michel de Montaigne* (i.e. not *The* Essays). What is also interesting is that this increases the reflexivity of the title, giving it the dual sense of 'Tastes *by* Michel de Montaigne', but also 'Tastes *of* Michel de Montaigne' – i.e. our tastes or samplings of him. And this reminds us of Montaigne's address 'To the Reader' where he describes his book as a means of 'nourishing' the memory of himself amongst his family and friends.

For Montaigne the gustatory overtones of his *Essays* are clear. He says of his working philosophy: 'I have lived long enough to give an account of the practice that has guided me so. For anyone who wants to taste it, I have tried it [*j'en ay faict l'essay*] like his cup-bearer.' In this way, we can perhaps see that Montaigne saw his project as less one of sceptical 'testing', and more of a 'tasting' or sampling of different subjects. And as such, it is a process that that never simply concludes, but matures. On the title page of the Bordeaux copy Montaigne scribbles: *Viresque acquirit eundo* – 'It gains strength as it proceeds', clearly a reference to Montaigne's growing confidence in his work, but also a thought familiar from his taste for 'old' wine that grows in strength and maturity.

The other word linked to wine that Montaigne relies on very heavily is the more commonplace word for taste, *goust* (the older spelling of the modern French *goût*). In the Bordeaux copy Montaigne uses 'goust' and its conjugations (*gouster*, *gousté*, etc.) on 106 occasions, a quite remarkable number of times. Moreover, if we add to this figure the number of times Montaigne uses the word in earlier editions only to subsequently erase it and replace it with another – such as 'appetite or 'sentiment' – as he perhaps becomes aware of his over-dependence on it, the number of instances increases to 146. As Montaigne's essays total around 430,000 words, this gives it a frequency of around once in every 3,000 words. If we look at Montaigne's *Travel Journal* we again find a remarkable proliferation of *goust*: thirty-six times in French, and seven times in its Italian form (including *gustevoli* – tasty): thus forty-three times in a work of 113,000 words (one in every 2,600).

By way of comparison, Francis Bacon's final edition of his own *Essays* of 1625 uses 'taste' only twice. And nowhere does Bacon use comparable synonyms such as 'flavour' or 'savour'. Bacon's essays are an eighth the length of Montaigne's (53,000 words), so that is to say he is only using it once every 26,500 words. Of course these figures are only approximations, but the point is that, although a comparable essayist such as Bacon is using the word 'taste', Montaigne is using it much more frequently – *up to ten times* more frequently – than anyone else.

Tasting therefore looms very large in Montaigne the *vigneron's* vocabulary, and hence very large in his mind. During his visits to the mineral baths of Europe, he thus extends his oenological faculties to the local waters. In Baden he finds it 'a little weak and flat, as if it had been poured back and forth a lot'. In Pisa he feels 'only a little sharpness on the tongue'. In Battaglia the water has 'a slight smell of sulphur, a little saltiness'. But in Plombières he pulls out all the stops:

> There are only two springs from which one can drink. That which issues from the eastern slopes and produces the bath that they call The Queen's Bath leaves a sort of sweet taste in the mouth like liquorice, without any aftertaste. But it seemed to Monsieur de Montaigne that if you paid special attention, you could detect a certain taste of iron. The other, which springs from the foot of the mountain opposite, of which Monsieur de Montaigne drank for only a day, has a little more bitterness, and one may discern in it the flavour of alum.

In Rome he even turns forensic chemist, having been given: 'a certain sort of drink that had precisely the taste and colour of almond milk', but goes on to detect '*quatre-semences-froides* in it' (i.e. the four cold seeds of cucumber, gourd, melon and pumpkin). Montaigne's winemaker's palate thus becomes extended to the wider world, to water and also obviously to food, about which he is very fussy.

In the *Essays* we see this aptitude manifest in a continuing preoccupation with taste. He talks of how the upper classes spend their time at table 'talking about the beauty of a tapestry, or the taste of the malmsey' (a Madeira wine). He tells of how the natives of South America drink a drink 'made of some root, and is the same colour as our claret wines . . . This beverage keeps only two or three days; it has a slightly sweet taste.' He tells how we can no more persuade ourselves that the lash of a whip tickles us than we can believe that a potion of aloes – a strong laxative – 'tastes' like a wine of Bordeaux.

But the notion of taste becomes essential to the development of Montaigne's essays, in the sense that they represent the extension of Montaigne's palate beyond wine, into a more abstract, metaphorical and philosophical realm, but one that ultimately returns him to the human body. Firstly, we see the natural extension of taste as a synonym for disposition, as in 'this depends on man's particular taste: mine is not adaptable to household management'. Neither does he think he possesses 'the taste for those lengthy offers of affection and service' required of public life. But through this Montaigne shows himself increasingly alert to the varieties of human experience. Writing of fish, he says that 'the great have pretensions of knowing how to prepare it; and indeed its taste is much more exquisite that that of flesh, at least to me'. And here the very important lesson for Montaigne is that we all have our own *particular* take on the world – quoting Horace on the dilemmas of entertaining:

> *Tres mihi convivae propre dissentire videntur,*
> *Poscentes vario multum diversa palato*

> Three guests I have dissenting at my feast
> Requiring each to gratify his taste
> With different food

But an awareness of this fact should, for Montaigne, be extended to politics and (by implication) religion. Varro calculated that trying to find the sovereign good gave rise to 288 sects. 'We fall to disputing, because one person differs from another as to what he hears, sees or tastes . . . a child tastes differently to a man of thirty, and the latter differently to a sexagenarian.' As early as 1564, around six years before he started work on the *Essays*, Montaigne makes notes on the flyleaves of his edition of Lucretius of passages relating to taste: *Quomodo fiat gustus* (How taste occurs); *Voluptas gustus tantum est in palato* (The pleasure of taste is in the palate alone). Whilst elsewhere Lucretius might insist that there is no new pleasure (*voluptas*) to be gained by living longer, here Montaigne, soon to take over the business of winemaking from his father, seems to be clearing a path to the idea that there is.

The idea of 'taste' thus allows Montaigne to explain how we have knowledge of the world, but, like our tastes in wine, it also explains how each of us differ. We think we have comprehensive knowledge of something, but we only have a taste. Thus of his education, he says that he 'has only tasted the outer crust of sciences in his childhood, and has retained only a vague general picture of them; a little of everything and nothing thoroughly'. All this goes towards satisfying his desire to explore what we might call the more subjective, or relativistic, side of human affairs – the fact that children might not like what we like, that people's attitude to death changes with time and company; the fact that we might have differing ideas about religion. And this faculty then spreads outwards, omnivorously extending his palate to the world around him. He sees travel as a means of 'tasting a perpetual variety of the forms of our nature'. He says he has never 'tasted' any tedious work and describes pedants as treating learning like birds, gathering grain, yet carrying it in their beak for their offspring without tasting it. Discussing wine glasses he says, 'I dislike all metal compared with a clear and transparent material. Let my eyes taste also according to their capacity.'

But what is also significant in the the context of Montaigne's experience as a *vigneron*, is that the late sixteenth century has been described as undergoing a 'mini Ice Age', in the period 1570–1630. This resulted in a series of terrible harvests, being particularly marked in the period in which Montaigne takes over his estate: the bad harvest of 1572 being followed by the heavy rains of 1573. The first essay that Montaigne writes – 'Of Idleness' – can thus be seen as not only a spiritual description – his reflections on the deaths of his best friend, his father, and his first-born child – but also a literal one, as his surveys the agricultural failures around him:

> In the same way that we see that idle land, if it is rich and fertile, becomes overgrown with a thousand kinds of wild and useless weeds, and that to set it to work we must sow it with certain kinds of seeds . . . so it is with minds.

But in the years after 1574 – i.e. in the years in which Montaigne seems to move away from his Stoic despondency – the weather and the wine harvest improve (and newly planted vines take five years to produce a full yield in any case). Thus in an early essay, 'The Taste [*Goust*] of Good and Evil Depends on the Opinion We Have of Them', Montaigne amplifies

Seneca's idea that 'everything depends on opinion' by adding the notion of taste to the equation; he then restates this idea more strongly in a later essay, 'We Taste [*Goustons*] Nothing Pure' (1578–80). And in the essay 'Of Practice' (1573–4), which starts from the idea that we need Stoicism as we cannot rehearse death, he nevertheless begins to speaks of those of the ancients who tried, in dying, 'to taste and savour it'. Although we cannot therefore experience death, we can nevertheless attempt to 'taste it' (*et de l'essayer*). Thus, even when he starts off intending to make a Stoic point, Montaigne is becoming acutely aware of the role of body and his sensing faculties.

But it is important to realize that Montaigne does not simply utilize this language in order to say what he thinks; through saying these things he finds out what he thinks and doesn't think. And as if to confirm this, in the changes that Montaigne makes to his use of *goust* in terms of deleting and replacing it, he often erases a usage that might seem strange to us, such as the use of 'taste' for an abstract situation (here the italics show the addition):

> But on how little depends our resoluteness in dying. The difference and distance of a few hours, the mere consideration of having company, makes our ~~taste~~ *apprehension* of it ~~completely~~ different.

Unlike the Stoics, who could live on an olive a day, Montaigne begins to explore the variety of human existence, its inconstancy, its vagueness, but also its richness. What is also interesting are those places where Montaigne simply deletes the word. In the 'Apology' he writes that:

> Things do not lodge in us in their form and essence . . . because if that were the case, we would receive them in

the same way: ~~the taste of~~ wine would be the same in the mouth of a sick man as in the mouth of a healthy one.

Montaigne deletes 'the taste of', to leave 'wine would be the same in the mouth' – a simple enough statement in our own sceptical, relativist age; but what is clear is that Montaigne's interest in 'taste' is paving the way for such an emphasis on the subjective, even if he then decides to discard it.

What we are in effect seeing is thus the *first pressing* of Montaigne's essays, in which the words flow freely from his pen. This then allows him – in a move that is epochal in the history of Western thought – to turn that language onto himself, in terms of his whole experience of life:

> Others sense the sweetness of contentment and prosperity. I feel it as well as they do, but not as it passes and slips away. One should study it, taste it, and ruminate upon it to give thanks to him who grants it to us.

> Everyone looks in front of himself; as for me, I look inside of myself, I have no concern but with myself, I consider myself continuously: I taste myself.

Montaigne's 'self-discovery', and his rejection of Stoicism, thus uses a language that comes instinctively to him as a winemaker. He then retrospectively prunes and ties back the language of his essays, grafting onto it a more intellectual register. But its first fruits are a spontaneous flowering.

As a consequence, it is not our attitude towards death that becomes the overwhelming issue for Montaigne, but our ability to *taste* life – to gourmandize it in effect. What is it that he sees in a horse, a book, a glass? He denies that it is an emotional attachment, and some might find his words a little cool – what about his wife, his daughter? But, as he goes on to explain, the grief surrounding such losses is easy to explain. If one were to speculate, one might say that what he seems to be saying is that, in their potential loss, it is the *experience* of them, his consciousness of them, the way they have a certain sensory or intellectual flavour – as he would say, a certain *'je ne sais quoi'* – which 'nourishes' in him a fear of losing them. And this becomes more evident the less emotionally complex the things are – a dog, a book, a glass. For in leaving them he will not be realizing himself, as in Stoicism, but losing something far more precious – the taste of life – something that does not divide us from the world, but brings us closer to it.

Of Experience

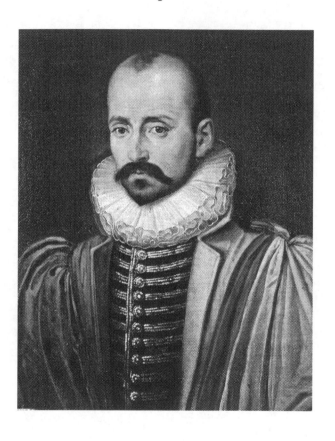

When I dance, I dance; when I sleep, I sleep; and when I am walking alone in a beautiful orchard, if my thoughts are sometimes elsewhere, for most of the time I bring them back to the walk, to the orchard, to the sweetness of this solitude, and to me.

Writing in one of his final essays towards the end of his life, Montaigne describes how, in 1586, 'a thousand different kinds of evil descended upon me, one after the other'. The Wars of Religion arrived on his doorstep, the nearby town of Castillon being besieged by the forces of the Catholic League. Thousands of soldiers poured into the area, bringing with them lawlessness and plunder: 'It comes to cure sedition, and is full of it; it would chastise disobedience, and gives an example of it . . . What a state we are in!' The homes of all his villagers were looted, and the agricultural reconstruction of the past century ripped up:

> The living had to suffer, so did those who were not yet born. They were pillaged, and myself as a consequence, even of hope, having ripped from them all they had to provide a living for themselves for many years to come.

The fields that once provided employment for a hundred men 'lay idle for a long time'.

And amidst this disaster, Montaigne found his own moderation the object of suspicion: 'The location of my house and the acquaintance of those in my neighbourhood presented me with one face; my life and actions with another.' And as a final blow, a plague 'of utmost severity' broke out within the besieged town, spreading up the hill to Montaigne, causing him and his family to flee his ancestral home, leaving it 'at the mercy of anyone who envied it'. For six months, he says, he served as guide to his family's homeless and pitiful caravan. But despite his own family's suffering, Montaigne says that it was the plight of the common people that grieved him the most. Of the villagers in his charge, 'not a hundredth part could save themselves':

> The grapes remained hanging on the vines, the principal wealth of this country, everyone indifferently preparing themselves and waiting for death that evening or the next day . . . I saw those who were afraid of being left behind, as in a horrible solitude, and I observed that in general they had no other care than for their burial. It distressed them to see the bodies spread over the fields, at the mercy of the creatures that freely infested them . . . Some, healthy, were already digging their graves; others lay down in them whilst still alive. And a labourer of mine pulled the earth over him with his hands and feet as he was dying. Was not this like covering himself up so that he might sleep more peacefully?

Yet from this terrible nightmare, Montaigne draws lessons. But not in terms of the stoical injunctions of the ancients. For he realizes that the people around him gain nothing by brooding on and anticipating death: 'If you do not know how to die, don't worry yourself: Nature will inform you what to do on the spot, plainly and adequately . . . don't bother your head about it.' Although he might have once thought, with Cicero, that 'the whole life of a philosopher is a meditation on death', Montaigne now changes his tune: 'Life should be an aim unto itself, a purpose unto itself'; 'Death is indeed the end, but not therefore the goal of life; it is its finish, its limit, but not therefore its object.' The Stoics, he finally declares, are 'the surliest sect'.

And turning his back upon the goal of *apatheia*, he condemns the political irresponsibility of those who 'harden themselves to view resolutely and without perturbation the ruin of their country'. Of himself, he says, 'I do not approve of that insensibility, which is neither possible nor desirable. I am not pleased to be sick, but if I am, I want to know that I am . . . I wish to feel it.' Such sensations he sees as part of the eternal inconstancy of life itself:

> The world is nothing but a perennial movement. All things are in a constant motion – the earth, the rocks of the Caucasus, the pyramids of Egypt – both with a common motion and their own. Constancy itself is nothing more than a more languid motion . . . I do not paint being, I paint transience . . .

But in closing the slim manual of Stoicism, Montaigne opens the large volume of life. He states in his later essays that it is 'living happily, not . . . dying happily that is the source of human contentment'. And whilst there are no 'skyhooks' on which to hang this morality, neither is there an abyss below: 'When I dance, I dance; when I sleep, I sleep.' Montaigne is perhaps the first writer in human history to lay his hand on human consciousness, though not, like Descartes, in an attempt to achieve certainty, but in an attempt to justify life on its own terms. Thinking may allow us to part company with ourselves – 'my thoughts are sometimes elsewhere' – but it is the task of philosophy to 'bring them back' to the human, to slow our walk through the orchard of life, and hold in our mouths, for as long as we can, the 'sweetness' and 'beauty' of living.

❧

Montaigne died at home on 13 September 1592. His final years were spent suffering from increasingly poor health, but he was tinkering with his essays till the end. In earlier days he had written: 'I have taken a road along which, without ceasing and without labour, I shall proceed as long as there is ink and paper in the world' – and to that undertaking he remained true.

He also lived to be a grandfather. On 27 May 1590 his daughter Léonor was married at the château to the thirty-year-old François de la Tour. After staying at the château for a month, they left for her new home in Saintonge. And on 31 March 1591 she gave birth to a daughter, baptized Françoise in honour of her mother.

Montaigne seemed to face death with a natural, unforced equanimity, writing in his final additions to the *Essays* of 'folding up my belongings and packing my bags'. His friend Estienne Pasquier described his final hours:

> He died in his house of Montaigne, where a quinsy [abscess] attacked his tongue in such a way that he remained three whole days full of understanding but unable to speak. As a result he was forced to have recourse to his pen to make his wishes known. And as he felt his end approaching, he wrote a little note asking his wife to summon a few gentlemen neighbours of his, so as to take leave of them. When they arrived he had mass said in his room; and when the priest came to the elevation of the *Corpus Domini*, this poor gentleman rose up as best he

could in his bed, with a desperate effort, hands clasped; and in his last action gave his spirit to God. Which was a fine mirror of his inmost soul.

His heart was buried in his local church of St-Michel-de-Montaigne whilst his body was placed in a tomb in the Eglise des Feuillants in Bordeaux. But a local historian added a final and, if true, perhaps more fitting memorial:

> The late Montaigne, author of the *Essays*, feeling the end of his days drawing near, got out of his bed in his nightshirt; taking his dressing gown, opened his study, had all his valets and other legatees called in, and paid them the legacies he had left them in his will, foreseeing the difficulties his heirs would make over paying the legacies.

Montaigne's reputation grew rapidly over the following years. Before he died he was visited by Anthony Bacon, whose younger brother Francis went on to imitate Montaigne in his own *Essays* of 1597. Montaigne's *Essays* were translated into Italian in 1590, English in 1603, Dutch in 1692, and German in 1753; and later into many other languages including Chinese, Japanese, Russian, Arabic and Greek. And readers and writers since then have found Montaigne the most fascinating and congenial of authors: Orson Welles describing him as 'the greatest writer of any time, anywhere'.

But perhaps the most sympathetic reader of Montaigne was Shakespeare, who quotes, almost verbatim, from John Florio's 1603 translation of Montaigne's description of the 'golden age' in 'Of Cannibals' in Gonzalo's address in *The Tempest*:

It is a nation, would I answer Plato,
that hath no kind of Trafficke,
no knowledge of Letters,
no intelligence of numbers,
no name of magistrate, nor of politike superiorities;
no use of service, of riches, or of povertie;
no contracts, no successions, no partitions,
no occupation but idle . . .
And were I king on't, what would I do? . . .

Florio, 1603

I' the commonwealth I would by contraries
Execute all things; for no kind of traffic
Would I admit; no name of magistrate;
Letters should not be known; riches, poverty,
And use of service, none; contract, succession,
Bourn, bound of land, tilth, vineyard, none;
No use of metal, corn, or wine, or oil;
No occupation; all men idle, all . . .

The Tempest (ii, i, 148-155)

The influence here seems incontrovertible, yet the wider depth of Shakespeare's debt to Montaigne is more difficult to discern. Some see *The Tempest* as the tip of a submerged iceberg of Montaignean influence. And one could see the whole of Shakespeare's tragic trajectory as an illustration of Montaigne's insistence on the paradoxical limitations of man's reason – i.e. Montaigne's words in the 'Apology' seem to sum up the essence of Shakespearean tragedy as well as any critic has ever done:

> . . . if it be that he alone, of all the creatures, has this freedom of imagination and this licence of thoughts, which represents to him both what is and what is not,

what pleases him, false and true, it is an advantage very highly bought . . .

Hamlet (1603), which in an early version featured a character called 'Montano', seems to be suffused with a similar scepticism: Hamlet's 'Your worm is your only emperor for diet' recalling Montaigne's the 'heart and life of a mighty and triumphant emperor is but the break-fast of a seely [blind] little worme'. And in his most famous soliloquy, Hamlet seems to achieve something like the dramatic equivalent of an essay, balancing opposing viewpoints as a means of exploring not only whether one should live or die, but also the nature of existence itself:

> To be, or not to be: that is the question:
> Whether 'tis nobler in the mind to suffer
> The slings and arrows of outrageous fortune,
> Or to take arms against a sea of troubles,
> And by opposing end them? To die: to sleep;
> No more; and by a sleep to say we end
> The heart-ache and the thousand natural shocks
> That flesh is heir to, 'tis a consummation
> Devoutly to be wish'd. To die, to sleep;
> To sleep: perchance to dream: ay, there's the rub;
> For in that sleep of death what dreams may come
> When we have shuffled off this mortal coil,
> Must give us pause: there's the respect
> That makes calamity of so long life.
> . . .
> Thus conscience does make cowards of us all;
> And thus the native hue of resolution
> Is sicklied o'er with the pale cast of thought,

And enterprises of great pith and moment
With this regard their currents turn awry,
And lose the name of action . . .

Hamlet (III, i, 56–90)

In overcoming Stoic, 'resolution' and senseless martial fortitude
with something like a more circumspect self-awareness,
Hamlet seems to undergo his own fall from his horse. And
whilst the ideas themselves might now seem commonplace,
prior to this, characters simply did not talk in this way – seeing
cognition and knowledge as central to human and therefore
dramatic experience. And Shakespeare's other tragic heroes
– Macbeth, Othello, King Lear – seem to be propelled along
a similar trajectory: they experience scepticism, intellectual
paralysis, and lose sight of the world, but at the same time
discover themselves.

Unsurprisingly, Montaigne is seen by many literary historians as
marking the inception of such forms of modern individualism
– epitomized in Hamlet's agonized anomie, and reaching their
apogee in Descartes. Virginia Woolf thus emphasizes the
detachment of Montaigne's mind from his body: 'brood[ing] over
the fire in the inner room of that tower which, though detached
from the main building, has so wide a view over the estate'. But it
could also be said that Montaigne represents the opposite, that in
looking inside himself, Montaigne is not looking for constancy or
escape, but rather something else – *company*:

> He who can pour into and mix up within himself the
> offices of friendship and companionship, let him do so . . .
> Let him soothe and caress himself, and, above all, govern

himself, respecting and fearing his reason and conscience,
so that he cannot without shame stumble in their presence.

Here, Montaigne demonstrates more than any other writer
that the very idea of the self is proof of our innate desire
for human contact – to have someone to talk to. And this is
literally proven by the fact that many of his essays, like large
sections of his *Travel Journal*, were dictated to a secretary –
Montaigne saying quite truthfully: 'I speak to my paper as I
speak to the first man I meet.'

And whilst self-knowledge is not something that can be
established with certainty, Montaigne nevertheless sees it as
a knowledge to which we can draw near. We should examine
ourselves not because we ourselves contain infallible truth, but
because – and this is the thought that sounds most strange to
us as modern readers – it is our own bodies, our own selves to
which we are closest:

> It is likely that if the soul knew anything, it would firstly
> know itself; and if it knew anything outside itself, it
> would be its body and shell before other things . . . We
> are nearer to ourselves than the whiteness of snow or the
> heaviness of a stone. If a man does not know himself,
> how can he know his functions and his powers?

The task of philosophy, therefore, is not to dig down to firmer,
more resolute foundations, or to rise up into the beyond, but
to show us where we already stand; not to shake off the body,
but to shake its hand.

And here Montaigne's circular tower undoubtedly served
as a means of focusing his thinking, though not in terms
of providing an escape from others, but in its shell-like
protection, its bedroom, toilet and library, constituting a *home*

– not a home from home but a home *within* a home. Unlike the itinerant Descartes, Montaigne *essays* himself only when he is most at home – near his books, his desk and chair, and the bell tolling above him – where he is closest to himself:

> The course of our desires ought to be circumscribed and restrained to a short limit of the nearest and most contiguous commodities; and moreover their course ought not to take off in a straight line, that ends elsewhere, but in a circle, of which the two points, by a short sweep, meet and terminate in ourselves. Actions that are carried on without this reflection – I mean, a *near* and essential reflection – such as those who are ambitious and avaricious, and so many more as run point-blank, and whose career always carries them before themselves, such actions, I say, are erroneous and sickly. [my italics]

Rather than indubitability, it is thus this localness, this 'home', that is Montaigne's central concern: 'We are never at home, we are always beyond ourselves'; the mind needs to be 'called home and confined within itself'; 'Every man rushes elsewhere and into the future, because no man has arrived at himself':

> It is an absolute perfection and virtually divine to know how to rightfully enjoy our being. We search for other conditions because we do not understand the use of our own, and go outside of ourselves because we do not know what it is like inside.

And on the last page of the *Essays*, Montaigne adds a final, soldierly retort to the attempt to distance ourselves from ourselves: 'Even on the highest throne in the world we are still sat on our backsides.'

What allows this sort of self-knowledge to have substance and texture, however, is Montaigne's experience as a *vigneron*. Whereas the mathematician Descartes expects to find truths that are as 'clear and distinct' as geometrical proofs, Montaigne exemplifies the idea of a patient, tentative, cumulative, sampling of life:

> I have a vocabulary all of my own. I 'pass the time', when it is bad and inclement; but when it is good, I do not wish it to pass, I re-taste it, I cling to it . . . This common phrase of pastime, and passing time, represents the usage of those wise sort of people who do not think they can do better with their lives than to let them run away and escape . . .

Through the faculty of taste, Montaigne is thus able to come even closer to himself (the verb that Montaigne uses here, *taster*, could also mean to touch). Such knowledge may not be 'clear and distinct' (for how can it be separate if we are in contact with it?), but this does not mean that it is not experienced at all. And with time, and practice, our understanding of it will deepen. We must educate our palates to understand ourselves; a process that requires time, that requires *life* – as he writes in one of the final additions to his text:

> Meditation is a powerful and rich study for those who know how to taste and exercise themselves vigorously; I would rather fashion my soul than furnish it. There is no activity that is either weaker or stronger, depending on the nature of the soul that is concerned in it, than that of entertaining one's own thoughts. The greatest minds make it their vocation, '*quibus vivere est cogitare*' [for whom to live is to think – Cicero].

Vivere est cogitare. For Descartes, our being is in doubt, the *cogito* is his attempt to prove its existence; but for Montaigne our existence is unproblematic: the question is our ability to appreciate it; to savour and taste it, to bring it near.

And for Montaigne such self-tasting is a process that never simply concludes, as we ourselves are changed by that we set out to sample: 'I have no more made my book than my book has made me.' We must therefore tend and cultivate our lives, in the same way that grapes are ripened on the vine:

> I want to increase it [life] in weight. I wish to arrest the rapidity of its flight by the rapidity of my grasp, and by my vigour in employing it make up for the speed of its flow. In proportion to the shortness of my possession of life, I must make it deeper and fuller.

It is not an abstract, final knowledge, but an evolving acquaintance, suggesting nearness, sweetness, nourishment. In 'Of Conversation', Montaigne remarks that through conversation 'we seek the truth', only to cross it out and write: 'we seek *what is*'.

Montaigne's final essay, 'Of Experience', thus offers an amazing catalogue of the tasting notes and textures of his own being. It is one of the most amazing texts in the history of Western philosophy, an unparalleled inventory of man's sensory station. Here, Montaigne turns his back on Stoicism and received ideas, which he sees as reiterating itself like a vine-stock – 'our opinions are grafted upon each another: the first serves as a stock for the second; the second to the third'. Instead, he looks to experience – a 'less dignified means', but one that brings us closer to Nature, whose 'laws are more successful than those we give ourselves':

For if we say that we lack authority to give credence for our testimony, we speak beside the point. For in my opinion, from the most ordinary, familiar and commonplace things, if we could see them properly, we could construct the greatest miracles in nature and the most wonderful examples, especially on the subject of human actions.

As he says in 'Of Physiognomy': 'We are each of us richer than we think.'

He goes on to sample his own particular constitution. How he needs a clean napkin as he makes little use of either knife or fork. How he is unable to sleep in the day, or eat between meals, or go to bed immediately after supper. And washing after a meal and curtains for his bed are 'quite essential'. He cannot take wine or water unmixed, and as for eating:

> I am not excessively keen either on salads or fruits, except melons. My father hated all kinds of sauces; I like them all. Eating too much bothers me; but I have no real knowledge that any kind of food disagrees with me, just as I do not notice whether the moon is full or waning, or whether it is autumn or spring. There are changes that take place in us, inconstant and unknown – radishes, for example, I first found agreeable, now disagreeable, now I like them again. In many ways I feel my stomach and appetite vary that way: I have changed back from white wine to claret, and then from claret to white again.

He eats greedily, bites his tongue; he likes to sleep with both legs raised.

And in the body of his writings, Montaigne adds colour and depth to this self-portrait. He is short and thickset, with a 'face not fat but full'. He has soft clear eyes, moderate nose, white and regular teeth (which he cleans every day with a napkin). He has a well-rounded head, pleasant open expression. He doesn't smell and his limbs are well set. He likes to wear black and white, like his father, but is a bit dapper: 'a cloak worn like a scarf . . . a neglected hose'. He is vigorous in his younger years, but can be jittery, easily distracted by a fly. He likes easy books, *The Decameron*, *The Kisses* of Johannes Secondus. He sees life as 'a material and corporeal movement, an action essentially imperfect, and irregular; I make it my business to serve it according to its nature'.

He writes a book that is the only one of its kind in the world, a book with a wild and eccentric plan. He scratches his ears. He hates bargaining. He wants death to find him planting his cabbages. He hates being interrupted on the toilet. He smells March violets in his urine, and goes at the same time each day, his bowels never failing to make their assignation 'which is

when I jump out of bed'. But we should not do as he has done, and become too attached to a particular place – in his case, the toilet a few steps down from his library. And yet in some of the fouler public conveniences, he asks, 'Is it not somewhat excusable to request a little more care and cleanliness?'

❧

But what is most important about Montaigne's awareness of himself, the vividness of his sense of his own acquaintance, is that it does not contradict his sense of a wider responsibility to society at large, the true distinction between himself and Descartes. Because Montaigne, perhaps more than any other writer, is preoccupied with what the link between our minds and our bodies can tell us about the nature of mankind more generally. 'If men were not different,' he notes, 'we would not be able to tell each other apart; if we were not similar, we wouldn't be able to recognize each other as men.' He comments that Seneca's stoical strictures are advantageous *'to the individual'* whereas Plutarch's writings are more 'gentle, and accommodating to social life'. He quotes approvingly Aristippus' statement that the principal benefit he gained from philosophy was that he could speak freely and openly to every man.

And it is partly through self-knowledge that this awareness of others is to be increased: 'Solitude of place, to say the truth, rather expands me and sets me at large outwardly.' He tells how we often find ourselves through contact with others; how he is excited 'by the opposition of another or by the warmth of my own speech'; 'the company, the very ring of my voice will draw more from my wit than I can find in it when I sound and exercise alone.' Studying others is thus a way of studying oneself:

By having trained myself from my youth to see a mirror of my own life in that of others, I have acquired a studious inclination in that direction, and when I am thinking of it, I let few things escape me that have a bearing on the matter – faces, humours, speeches.

Self-knowledge is thus tied up with our knowledge of other people: through it we gain a glimpse of 'the universal pattern of the human', that which is common to us all.

But perhaps the true consequences of Montaigne's sense of the interrelatedness of ourselves are suggested by his essay 'Of Cruelty', which immediately precedes his 'Apology for Raymond Sebond'. The essay starts by asking what is the conventional definition of virtue: the answer being that which requires 'difficulty and struggle', particularly in the withstanding of the pleasures of the body by the soul. In this sense we might say God is just, all-powerful, but we would not call him virtuous: his justice and goodness are dispensed at his ease. But for humans, virtue 'refuses ease for a companion', preferring the rough and thorny road to the mild and gentle path.

Montaigne then stops himself in his tracks and says: 'I have come this far without any trouble', but then asks whether this 'difficult' virtue is true of the finest souls, such as Socrates, who seemed to be endowed with a 'simple and affable nature' and with an instinctive distaste for evil. And then Montaigne turns to himself, for what he sees as his main virtue – his hatred of cruelty – is not something that he arrives at by reason, but simply arises in him instinctively:

> The good that is in me . . . is in me by the chance of my birth . . . Amongst other vices I cruelly hate cruelty, both by nature and by judgement, as the most extreme

of all the vices. But it is to a point of such softness that I cannot see a chicken's neck twisted without being distressed, and I cannot bear to hear the crying of a hare between the teeth of my dogs, even though the chase is a violent pleasure.

But this empathy is not reserved for animals, but is part of his sympathetic nature more generally: 'I am very tenderly compassionate for the afflictions of others.' In Basel he sees a poor man's little boy being operated on for a rupture, and, he records, 'being handled very roughly by the surgeon'. He cannot watch executions – 'no matter how just they may be' – without blinking. He pities the dying more than the dead, and is easily moved to tears. But what is important about Montaigne's confession of unmanly 'softness' is that it is not based on an idea of justice, or liberality, but simply arises from his proxemic and behavioural response to the punishment of others. Irrespective of how 'just' an execution may be, it is the *process* of it that he finds upsetting. And in a final addition to the *Essays*, he confesses that 'nothing provokes my tears except tears, and not only those that are genuine, but whatever their kind, whether feigned or painted'. It is for this reason that tragedy moves us: the lamentations of Dido and Ariadne affect us even though we do no believe in them: 'It is a sign of a harsh and unyielding nature to feel no emotion at such things.' It is not the beliefs or the circumstances behind grief that upsets him, but the witnessing of grief itself.

Montaigne's response to cruelty is important because, as he says, he lives 'in a time when we abound in incredible examples of this vice'. But this has not, he says, 'by any means habituated me to it'. Returning to animals, he says that the spectacle of the stag, bloodied, breathless and exhausted, surrendering itself to his pursuers 'has always affected me most unpleasantly'. He says he hardly ever catches an animal alive without returning it to the fields, and tells how Pythagoras would buy fish and birds from their vendors in order to do the same. What is important here is that Montaigne offers no higher theoretical arguments in support of his sympathy: it is not the thought that the animal necessarily has sentience or sensation, or rights, but rather the 'piteous cry' of the animal that affects him: 'These are the foundations of our grief.'

One might conclude from this that Montaigne's morality is merely a liberal one, lamenting man's innate cruelty but offering no real answer to how to live our lives. But this sense of the beholdenness of ourselves to others (and also of others' beholdenness to ourselves) reaches a climax in his penultimate essay, 'Of Physiognomy', in which he faces up to and faces down the unfaithful cruelty of the age in which he lives.

The essay is in part a meditation on the power of beauty – 'a quality that grants power and advantage' – but more deeply a demonstration of Montaigne's insight that 'there is nothing so unsociable and sociable as man: the one by his vice, the other by his nature' – that is to say, human relations are not abstract, but visible, tangible things. And by way of illustration he tells how during the civil wars a neighbour attempted to seize his house. Despite its vulnerable location, and unlike his father, Montaigne added no fortifications to it, making an attack on it 'a cowardly and treacherous business . . . it is not shut to anyone that knocks'. Its only sentinel was an aged porter, 'whose function is not so much to defend his door as to offer it with more grace and decorum'. And it was this unguardedness, this trusting nature, that a neighbour planned to turn to his own advantage:

A person once made a plan to seize my house and myself. His scheme was to arrive alone at my door and urgently request to be let in. I knew him by name and had reason to trust him as a neighbour, and to some extent an ally. I had the doors opened to him, as I do to everyone. Here he was completely terrified, his horse out of breath and all exhausted. He entertained me with this fable: that he had just met with an enemy of his half a league away . . . I tried naively to comfort, reassure and refresh him. Soon after, four or five of his soldiers arrived, with the same bearing and fright, in order to come in; and then more and more after them, well equipped and well armed, until there were twenty-five or thirty, pretending to have the enemy at their heels. This mystery was beginning to arouse my suspicion. I was not ignorant in what sort of age I was living, how my house might be envied, and knew several examples of others of my acquaintance who had suffered the same misadventure. However, thinking that there was nothing to be gained in having begun to be pleasant without going through with it, and being unable to disentangle myself without ruining everything, I abandoned myself to the most natural and simple course, as I do always, and gave orders for them to be let in . . .

These men stayed on horseback in my courtyard, the leader with me in my living room, who had not wanted to have his horse stabled, saying that he had to return as soon as he had news of his men. He saw himself master of this enterprise, and nothing now remained but its execution. He has often said to me since, for he was not afraid to tell this story, that my face and my frankness had wrestled the treachery from him. He remounted his horse, his men keeping their eyes on him for some signal he might give them, very astonished to see him leave and abandon his advantage.

And then Montaigne relates a similar incident, when he was ambushed by a band of masked men in the forest of Villebois whilst on his way to Paris in 1588, his strong-box seized, his servants and horses divided up. But then whilst he was being led off to a distance of 'two or three musket shots', Montaigne obviously fearing the worst,

> a sudden and altogether unexpected change came over them. I saw the leader returning to me with gentler language, going to the trouble of searching for my scattered articles among his men . . . even my strong-box . . . The most conspicuous of them, who took off his mask and let me know his name, repeated to me several times that I owed this deliverance to my face, and the liberty and firmness of my speech, which showed that I did not deserve such misfortune, and he asked me to assure him of similar treatment.

What foils his neighbour's coup and the attempt to rob him is the simple, open power of Montaigne's face. It is this and the 'freedom and firmness' of his speech that delivers him. He is saved not by their mercy, but by his own honesty – in the latter instance he says that 'I openly confessed to them at the beginning to what party I belonged and what road I was taking'. And it is this that precipitates a matching honesty in his assailant: he 'took off his mask and let me know his name'. Moreover, his erstwhile enemy then becomes his ally, forewarning him of another ambush that would have befallen him the next day, and asking Montaigne to assure him of 'similar treatment' if the tables were turned.

'If my face did not answer for me,' observes Montaigne, 'if men did not read the innocence of my intention in my eyes and in my voice, I should not have survived so long without quarrels and without offence.' Our conduct and our demeanour go before us, and exert a power over others. Moreover, in this cynical, sceptical, Machiavellian age, where all appearances are to be mistrusted, Montaigne attempts to show that in the primal scene of knowledge – a man meeting another man – certain values still inhere: 'Pure naturalness and truth, in whatever age, still find an opportunity and an opening.' 'The face may offer a weak security, but it counts for something all the same.' Appearances may sometimes be deceptive, but as Montaigne says elsewhere: 'there is nothing useless in Nature, not even uselessness itself'. His unwillingness to appear inhospitable and uncharitable to his assailant compels his assailant to do the same; in Montaigne's phraseology, it 'wrestles' the treachery from his hands. We may mistrust, but we cannot totally relinquish our beholdenness to the carriage and gesture of others. And it is through our gestures and the 'freedom and firmness' of our speech that this trust is to be re-affirmed.

Montaigne's anecdote about his house thus offers an alternative foundation to that provided by Descartes: where truth, or more importantly trust, is re-established, not through an escape from others into a rarefied form of reason, but through a closer reassertion of morality, man-to-man. Vice thrives on distance: Montaigne quotes Lucretius on the callous pleasure of seeing someone far from shore, struggling against the storm. And in Rome he notes that the brotherhood of 'gentlemen and prominent people' that accompany public executions hide themselves behind white linen masks. And these distances are augmented by the artificial distances of money, religion and power: Alexander has Betis' heels pierced and him dragged through the streets; he doesn't do it himself.

And in his essays more generally, Montaigne explores the power of human presence in moral life. He tells how Augustus, learning of Cinna's conspiracy, had him brought before him, placed in a chair provided for him, and then told him his knowledge of the conspiracy, only to then forgive him, asking: 'Let us see whether I have shown better faith in sparing your life or you in receiving it.' Alexander, receiving a letter informing him that Philip, his physician, had been paid by Darius to poison him, had Philip similarly brought before him, and made to read the letter, whilst drinking down the medicine that Philip had prepared. Caesar registered shock at Pompey's death, not in being told of it, but only when he was presented with his head.

For Montaigne, human proximity is thus at the heart of morality: 'to enter a breach, conduct an embassy, govern a people' are commonly praised, and piety is easily faked: 'Its essence is abstract and hidden; its forms easy and ceremonial.' But 'to hold pleasant and reasonable conversation with oneself and one's family, to not let go of oneself or be false to oneself, this is rarer and more difficult to achieve'; 'Few men have been admired by their own household.' But such proximity is also the basis of happiness itself: 'the recognition of our parents, our children and our friends'. And, more generally, Montaigne sees society as improved by gregariousness, and shared social space. Recalling the role of drama in antiquity, he remarks that 'well governed polities take care to assemble and bring together their citizens not only for the solemn duties of devotion, but also for sports and entertainments. Sociability and friendliness are thus increased.'

And Montaigne's belief in the importance of proximity to morality would seem to be supported by scientific evidence. In a series of famous experiments carried out at Yale in the 1960s, the psychologist Stanley Milgram set about exploring people's 'obedience' to figures of authority, particularly in situations which seemed to contradict their moral sense. Participants were recruited and told by a white-coated 'experimenter' to administer electric shocks to a 'pupil' (actually played by an actor) in another room depending upon their answers to certain memory tests. Participants were told to increase the level of shocks from 'Intense Shock' to 'Danger: Severe Shock' and finally to 'XXX' as the pupils continued to get their answers wrong. Milgram found that 65 per cent of people – both men and women – were prepared to administer shocks up to the highest level, a far higher figure than anyone had predicted.

But what was also interesting was how the proximity of the victims affected the participants' responses. The first set of experiments saw the pupil as relatively isolated, only able to communicate by briefly banging on the wall. But as the 'pupil' was moved nearer, firstly through verbal feedback, then into the same room, and finally into a position where the subject was instructed to place the the pupil's hand on the electrode, the percentage of subjects prepared to administer the highest shock declined to 30 per cent. Moreover, when the proximity of the experimenter was decreased, and their instructions were conveyed only via telephone, the rate of compliance sank to 21 per cent.

Obviously Milgrim's findings suggest some depressing conclusions, for some perhaps implying a despair about human relations. But they also reveal something else: that our willingness, and also our reluctance to hurt others is bound up with our proxemic beholdenness – i.e. our closeness to the experimenter or the victim. And that in order to make sure that we are properly morally informed about a situation, we need to make sure that the authority for and the consequences of our actions – the experimenter and the victim – are both with us in the same room.

As he ends the *Essays*, Montaigne seems to offer a similar lesson, and a similar sort of answer to his original conundrum: whether it is better to defy or prostrate ourselves before a conquering force; whether we should despair of social relations. The answer he gives is a moral rather than a tactical one, however: that rebuilding morality involves restoring the proxemic beholdenness of men. At the heart of Montaigne's morality is something that the 'great and tedious debates about the best form of society' and the ideal polities 'feigned by art' invariably tend to ignore:

> . . . that the society of men will hold and bind itself together, at whatsoever cost. In whatever position they are placed, they pile up and arrange themselves by moving and shuffling about, just as a group of objects thrown into a bag find their own way to join and fit together, often better than they could have been arranged deliberately.

A certain 'necessity reconciles and brings men together'. We are more beholden to each other than we know. Our language and our theories may seek to escape this, in attempting to find a mooring beyond ourselves, but we risk losing hold of what lies in front of us. Montaigne's intuitive awareness of the imitative power of behaviour – the 'mirror neurons' that serve as an antidote to our selfish genes – shows that we are already engaged in a two-way conversation with others: that we are not powerless over their behaviour, nor are they indifferent to ours. If we are looking for a reason for doing good – as Montaigne's experience in holding on to his house suggests – it might simply be that in doing so, others are more likely to feel the same; and that in doing things to others, we are doing things to ourselves.

It is near zero as I set out from Bordeaux, the sun barely visible above a cold white horizon. As I travel east the land outstretches: the smaller fields opening onto larger ones; the houses dispersing. But the earth stays sleeping. The leaves and the branches are silent, only the pruned vine stocks seem to shake their fists against the sky.

After an hour I cross the river – only a few hundred metres now – and skirt Castillon, obeying the satellite navigation's bland Calvinism, and start to climb. Dogs bark. A farmer washes his buckets. The road levels and I stop and turn left, then curve right into the village, past the school and the church, and then into the grounds of the château. The electronic display reports the exact location: 44°52'33"N, 0°01'47"E. I go into the ticket office, buy a ticket and a bottle of wine, and walk the few hundred yards to the tower. In the woods a jay laughs his cold corvine laugh.

The attendant unlocks the door and lets me in, turning on the lights. Through the door to the right is the chapel: its halogen heater lending a hand to the spirit. Above is the bedroom and its four-poster bed. And finally I continue up the steps, past the toilet with its tiny window, and duck through the door into the library, wider and lighter than you might think.

Empty of books, it now holds only some fading mementos – a plaque, a picture, a statue; a pair of dusty saddles; a table and a chair that Montaigne possibly never used. But as I slowly revolve, gazing up at the constellations of inscriptions above me, I wonder about the others who have done the same: opened this door, looked from this window, touched this wall – all in search of our oldest superstition, something irrefutable yet undefined.

That the fact that Montaigne stood here means something. But not in terms of some abstract universal – some spirit of the place – but something more local, proximate, private and domestic, something truer to Montaigne and to ourselves. That if I reach out my hand I can almost touch his; that we are separated by only a thin sliver of time. And that these coordinates, more than any other, possess a sort of moral gravity. And the simplest proof of this is the fact that I am here.

Montaigne's tower is thus unique in preserving the personal space of one of the greatest writers of all time, but also a writer for whom personal presence was part of the story that he wished to tell. As he looks into our futures he sees a natural phenomenon on the verge of extinction: a sense that what we are is somehow between us; an awareness of others as integral to ourselves. And these round walls seem to preserve this betweenness, making space tangible and tastable: a thickening of the invisible, a sense of space as a bringing together rather than a pulling apart. In the face of the divisions and distances of modernity, Montaigne reminds us that our deepest, nearest, human needs – issues of human contentment – revolve around a tight orbit, sometimes no larger than this room. And to this end he tries to return philosophy to its roots – as *philo-sophia*: not simply a love of wisdom, but a friendship with wisdom, a desire to get close to it, to meet it and embrace it as a friend. In trying to reach beyond our capacities – to make 'the handful bigger than the hand . . . straddle higher than our legs' – we risk overlooking the intimate but no less intimidating distances between us.

And as if to affirm this, inscribed on the walls of his study are the signatures of hundreds of visitors – anxious to see the place where Montaigne worked, the floor on which he walked, the room in which he slept, and the toilet where he reminded himself that he was stubbornly, frustratingly, painfully, but ultimately – to his great relief – also cut from the universal pattern of the human. Yet simultaneously these signatures also suggest a desire to connect with our own bearing and presence – to meet with Montaigne in order to meet and touch base with ourselves. To announce – as some wag has signed himself on the wall – 'Moi!'

But this is something that Montaigne knew all along. After circling this space, and attempting to imagine what life was like for Montaigne – hearing the shouts of château life alongside the chatter of birdsong outside – I open my copy of the *Essays* and turn to the beginning, where Montaigne seems to open the door before we have knocked, and in his words 'To the Reader' seems to address each of ourselves:

> You have here a book of good faith, reader. It tells you at the outset that I have here proposed to myself no other aim but a domestic and private one. I have here had no consideration for your service or my glory. My powers are not capable of such a design. I have dedicated it to the particular commodity of my family and friends, so that when they have lost me (which they must do soon), they will here retrieve some traits of my conditions and humours, and by that nourish entirely and vividly the knowledge they had of me. Had my intention been to seek the world's favour, I should have adorned myself with borrowed beauties, or have strained to draw myself up into my best posture. I want to be seen here in my

simple, natural, and ordinary manner, without exertion or artifice: for it is myself I paint. My defects are there to be read to the life, and my natural form, so far as public decency permits me. If I had been placed among those nations which they say still live under the sweet liberty of the laws of nature, I assure you I would have most willingly have painted myself entirely and fully naked.

So, reader, I am myself the matter of my book. There's no reason you should employ your leisure on a subject so frivolous and vain.

So farewell. Montaigne, this first day of March, fifteen hundred and eighty.

Nowhere is Montaigne's witty humility more evident than here, as he invites us inside, yet asks us to leave our critical sword in the hall. Yet what is remarkable about this preface is the way it reaches out to the reader – almost literally – across time and space (as he says of his book and himself elsewhere: 'Who touches one touches the other'; and he said to Henry III, 'My book and I are one'). For here, Montaigne forsakes the traditional formality of dedications and uses the more intimate '*tu*'. He also keeps the present tense and an almost oral present indicative constantly to the fore (not simply this book, but this book *here*). And rather than aiming at a satisfying a universal objective, 'the world's favour', Montaigne's aim is more local, recording his traits and his humours for his 'family and friends'. For Descartes, his book is the Truth, the work of a 'single master'. For Montaigne, the book is the site of a social event, the meeting of writer and reader, of Michel de Montaigne and you.

But what is also significant is Montaigne's description of it as a book of 'good faith' ('*bonne foi*'). For by 'good faith' Montaigne brings in a rich set of associations: Catholic ones, where good faith saves the soul of someone who is unable to receive the sacraments; legal ones, where good faith is an important component of the law of contract; but also the idea of marriage, seen as a relationship of love, but also of trust and fidelity.

And intimately linked to the idea of *bonne foi* was a handshake or handclasp, an image of trust and welcome that went back to antiquity, often in the image of a meeting between the living and the dead, but also standing for, as one historian puts it, for 'an end of hostility, an act of friendship, a pledge of faith'. A soldier in Froissart's *Chronicles* thus offers his hand to another 'to swear his faith' ('*pour faire jurer sa foi*'), a use that is clearly linked to other rituals involving hands and faithfulness, such as the 'handfasts' of betrothal or pledging feudal obedience to a lord, or vows made using a lady's glove or a knight's gauntlet, or oaths sealed by putting one's hand on a book.

In Montaigne's time, we can see this identification of 'good faith' with a handclasp in printers devices, such as on Bacon's *Advancement of Learning* of 1624, which shows the meeting of two hands above the Latin motto *Bona fides*, or that of the Parisian printer Nicolas de Sercy, where two clasping hands are shown surmounted by a crown, along with the motto *La bonne Foy couronneé*. But perhaps it is most clearly displayed in emblem books, like the *Emblemata* of Andrea Alciato, published in multiple editions between 1531 and 1621 (and most probably read by Montaigne). Here good faith is pictured as a relationship between Truth (seen carrying a book and nearly naked), joining hands with Honour, and both of them joined together by True Love (an infant boy). The motto reads: 'These images constitute good faith, which the reverence due to Honour fosters, Love nourishes, Truth brings to birth.'

And so for Montaigne, 'good faith' is more than simply truth, as truth is only one corner of the triangle, but is rather constituted by the meeting of all three – honour, truth, and true love: reader, writer and book. And as if to seal this, Montaigne presents himself before you in person, in the face-to-face oral dignity of the French nobility, addressing you, 'the Reader', in person, saying he is himself the 'matter' of his book, and placing his book – and his hand – in your hand.

Select Bibliography

Renderings of Montaigne are my own, although interested readers are directed to the two very fine English translations in print: Donald M. Frame's *The Complete Works of Montaigne* (New York: Everyman, 2003; first published 1957), and Michael Screech's *The Complete Essays* (Harmondsworth: Penguin, 1993). Online editions of the *Essais* and the *Journal de Voyage* may be found at http://humanities.uchicago.edu/orgs/montaigne/, and John Florio's and Charles Cotton's translations may also be easily found online. The secondary material on Montaigne is voluminous: below I have tried to indicate materials that may be of interest to the general reader as well as discharging some of my numerous debts.

Abecassis, Jack I. 'Montaigne's Aesthetics of Seduction and the Constitution of the Modern Subject', *Montaigne Studies*, 2 (1990), 60–81.

Alciato, Andreas. *Emblematum libri II* (1556), p. 154 for the symbol of 'bonne foi' (reproduced by permission of University of Glasgow Library, Dept of Special Collections).

Ariès, Philippe. *Western Attitudes Towards Death from the Middle Ages to the Present*, trans. Patricia M. Ranum (Baltimore: Johns Hopkins University Press, 1974), pp. 1–25 for Ariès's concept of 'tamed death'.

Bacon, Francis. *The Essays*, ed. John Pitcher (Harmondsworth:

Penguin, 1985), p. 108 for the atheism of Leucippus, Democritus
and Epicurus.

Baumgartner, Frederic J. *From Spear to Flintlock: History of War
in Europe and the Middle East to the French Revolution* (Santa
Barbara: Greenwood Press, 1991), p. 187 for Don John of
Austria's advice on arquebus firing.

Behringer, Wolfgang. 'Weather, Hunger and Fears: Origins of the
European Witch Hunts in Climate, Society and Mentality',
German History, 13 (1995), 1–27 for the mini Ice Age of the late
sixteenth century.

Bloch, Marc. *Feudal Society*, trans. L. A. Manyon (Chicago:
University of Chicago Press, 1961), vol. I, pp. 145–6 for
handclasps in feudal society.

Bomford, Kate. 'Friendship and Immortality: Holbein's
Ambassadors Revisited', *Renaissance Studies*, 18 (2004), 544–81
for Holbein's *Ambassadors* as a representation of friendship.

Boutcher, Warren. 'Marginal Commentaries: The Cultural
Transmission of Montaigne's *Essais* in Shakespeare's England',
in *Montaigne et Shakespeare: vers un nouvel humanisme*, ed. Jean-
Marie Maguin (Montpellier, Société Française Shakespeare &
Université de Paris III, 2003), 13–27; p. 14 for critics' views of the
'hidden iceberg' of Montaigne's influence on Shakespeare.

Briggs, Robin. *Witchcraft and Neighbours* (Harmondsworth: Penguin,
1998), p. 8 for the number of European witchcraft accusations.

Bullinger, Heinrich. *The Christen State of Matrimonye* (1541),
fol. 75r–v for Protestant advice on the conduct of wives and
daughters.

Burke, Peter. *Montaigne* (Oxford: Oxford University Press, 1981)

Calvin, Jean, Battles, Ford Lewis and Hugo, Andre Malan. *Calvin's
Commentary on Seneca's De Clementia* (Leiden: E. J. Brill, 1969),
p. 53 for Calvin's commentary on Seneca.

Cervantes, Miguel. *Don Quixote*, trans. Tobias Smollet (New York:
Barnes and Noble, 2004), p. 328 for Don Quixote's treatise on
armaments.

Charlton, Walter. *Physiologia Epicuro-Gassendo-Charletonia* (1654), p.505 for Charlton's scepticism about animals' interiority.

Clark, Willen, B. trans. and ed. *A Medieval Book of Beasts: The Second-Family Bestiary* (Woodbridge: Boydell Press, 2006), pp. 43, 130 for the spiritual lessons of weasels and beavers.

Clarke, Desmond M. *Descartes: A Biography* (Cambridge: Cambridge University Press, 2006), p. 180 for the description of Descartes as a 'reclusive, cantankerous, and oversensitive loner'.

Davis, Natalie Zemon. *Society and Culture in Early Modern France* (Stanford: Stanford University Press, 1975), pp. 152–87 for 'rites of violence' during the Wars of Religion.

Dekker, Elly and Lippincott, Kristen. 'The Scientific Instruments in Holbein's Ambassadors: A Re-Examination', *Journal of the Warburg and Courtauld Institutes*, 62 (1999), 93–125 for the astronomical instruments in Holbein's *Ambassadors*.

Delbrück, Hans. *The Dawn of Modern Warfare*, trans. Walter J. Renfroe, Jr. (Nebraska: University of Nebraska Press, 1990), vol. IV, p. 43 for the slaughter at the battle of Pavia.

Desan, Phillipe. 'The Montaigne Project', an interview with Desan in *Fathom* magazine (www.fathom.com/feature/122610/index.html) for the different inks in Montaigne's line 'because it was him; because it was me'.

Descartes, René. *Selected Philosophical Writings*, trans. John Cottingham, Robert Stoothoff and Dugald Murdoch (Cambridge: Cambridge University Press, 1988)

Dewald, Jonathan. *Aristocratic Experience and the Origins of Modern Culture: France 1570–1715* (Berkeley: University of California Press, 1993), pp. 55–6 for Monluc's condemnation of firearms.

Epictetus, *Enchiridion*, trans. George Long (New York: Dover, 2004), pp. 2–3 for quotations (very slightly modified) from Epictetus.

Erasmus, Desiderius, *Enchiridion militis christiani* (*The Handbook of the Christian Soldier*), trans. Charles Fantazzi, *The Collected Works of Erasmus*, ed. John W. O'Malley (Toronto: University

of Toronto Press), vol. LXVI, p. 84 for Erasmus's literate
humanism.

Erasmus, Desiderius. *De Utraque Verborem Ac Rerum Copia* (*On
Copia of Words and Ideas*), trans. Donald B. King and H. David
Rix (Milwaukee: Marquette University Press, 1963), pp. 38–41 for
Erasmus's delight at receiving a letter.

Flaubert, Gustave, *Selected Letters*, trans. J. A. Cohen (London:
Weidenfeld and Nicolson, 1950), p. 115 for Flaubert's eulogy to
Montaigne.

Ford, Franklin L. 'Dimensions of Toleration: Castellio, Bodin,
Montaigne', *Proceedings of the American Philosophical Society*, 116
(1972), 136–9, p. 137 for the translation of Castellio's dedication of
the Bible to Henry II.

Frame, Donald. *Montaigne: A Biography* (London: Hamish
Hamilton, 1965), pp. 272–3 for the quotations from the English
and Spanish ambassadors; p. 305 for the descriptions of
Montaigne's death; and *passim*.

Friedrich, Hugo. *Montaigne*, trans. Dawn Eng, ed. Philippe Desan
(Berkeley: University of California Press, 1991)

Froissart, Jean. *Chroniques*, ed. S. Luce, G. Raynaud, Léon Mirot
and Albert Mirot (Paris: Société de l'histoire de France,
1869–1975), vol. XI, p. 143 for a soldier swearing his faith with a
handclasp.

Gallese, V., Fadiga, L., Fogassi, L. and Rizzolatti, G. 'Action
Recognition in the Premotor Cortex', *Brain*, 119 (1996), 593–609
for the discovery of mirror neurons.

Hall, Edward T. *The Hidden Dimension* (New York: Doubleday,
1966), p. 121 for Hall's description of the gravitational pull
between bodies.

Harrison, Peter. 'The Virtues of Animals in Seventeenth-Century
Thought', *Journal of the History of Ideas*, 59 (1998), 463–84, pp.
466–7 for Jacob ibn-Zaddick's relating of human attributes to
animals.

Harrison, William. *The Description of England*, ed. Georges Edelen

(New York: Dover, 1994), p. 130 for the different varieties of wine on offer in Elizabethan England.

Herbert, George. *The English Poems*, ed. Helen Wilcox (Cambridge: Cambridge University Press, 2007), p. 23 for Herbert's 'The Agonie'.

Hoffmann, George. *Montaigne's Career* (Oxford: Oxford University Press, 1998), p. 76 for Montaigne's decision to withdraw La Boétie's *On Voluntary Servitude*; and *passim* for Montaigne's life and writing practice.

Hoffmann, George. 'Anatomy of the Mass: Montaigne's "Of Cannibals"', *Publications of the Modern Language Association* 117 (2002), 207–21 for the links between Amerindian religion and Catholicism.

Holt, Mack P. *The French Wars of Religion, 1562–1629* (Cambridge: Cambridge University Press, 2005)

Irving, David. *Memoirs of the Life and Writings of George Buchanan* (Edinburgh: William Blackwood, 1807), pp. 106–7 for the Latin text of Buchanan's poem 'Coming to France'.

Jensen, Kristian. 'The Humanist Reform of Latin and Latin Teaching', in *The Cambridge Companion to Renaissance Humanism*, ed. Jill Kraye (Cambridge: Cambridge University Press, 1996) 63–81, p. 65 for Johannes Santritter's praise of eloquence.

La Boétie, Etienne de. *Oeuvres*, ed. Paul Bonnefon (Paris: J. Rouam, 1892)

La Boétie, Etienne de. *Poemata*, ed. and trans. James S. Hirstein and Robert D. Cottrell, *Montaigne Studies*, 3 (1991), p. 29 for La Boétie's description of the youthful Montaigne's 'fiery energy'.

La Framboisière, Nicolas-Abraham de. *Oeuvres* (1669), p. 87 for the rankings of French wines.

La Marche, Olivier de. 'L'estat de la Maison du Duc Charles Le Hardy', in *Nouvelle Collection des Mémoires pour servir à l'Histoire de France*, ed. J. F. Michaud and J. J. F. Poujoulat (Paris, 1837), ser. i, vol. III, p. 589 for the 'assay' of wine in a noble household.

Le Roy Ladurie, Emmanuel. *The French Peasantry, 1450–1660*, trans. Alan Sheridan (Aldershot: Scolar Press, 1987), pp. 130–31 for Bordeaux wine exports in the late sixteenth century.

Legros, Alain, *Essais sur Poutres: Peintures et Inscriptions Chez Montaigne* (Paris: Klincksieck, 2000), pp. 317–22 for Montaigne's erasing of Lucretius' *Nec nova vivendo procuditur ulla voluptas*.

Leyser, Karl. *Communications and Power in Medieval Europe: The Carolingian and Offonian Centuries*, ed. Timothy Reuter (London: Hambledon Press, 1994). p.191 for handclasps as a pledge of faith.

Machiavelli, Niccolò. *The Prince*, trans George Bull (Harmondsworth: Penguin, 1993), p. 56 for rulers needing to imitate foxes and lions.

Machyn, Henry. *The Diary of Henry Machyn*, ed. John Gough Nichols (London: Camden Society, 1848), p. 289 for the wine at William Harvey's daughter's christening.

Malebranche, Nicolas. *The Search After Truth (Recherche de la vérité)*, trans. Thomas M. Lennon and Paul J. Olscamp (Cambridge: Cambridge University Press, 1997), pp. 494–5 for Malebranche's scepticism about animal sentience.

Matthews, John Hobson. ed. 'Margam Abbey Muniments: Select Documents to 1568', in *Cardiff Records* (1901), vol. III, no. 1102 for the local rights of the Earl of Pembroke.

Milgram, Stanley. *Obedience to Authority: An Experimental View* (New York: Harper & Row, 1974).

Mirandola, Pico della. *On the Dignity of Man; On Being and the One; Heptaplus*, trans. Charles Wallis, Paul Miller and Douglas Carmichael (Indianapolis: Bobbs-Merrill, 1965), pp. 6–7 for Pico's humanistic optimism.

Monluc, Blaise de. *The Habsburg–Valois Wars and the French Wars of Religion*, ed. Ian Roy (London: Longman, 1971), p. 221 for Monluc's injury at the siege of Rabastens.

Montaigne, Michel de. *Essais de Michel de Montaigne: Texts original de 1580 avec les variantes des editions de 1582 et 1587*, ed.

R. Dezeimeris and H. Barckhausen, 2 vols (Bordeaux: Feret, 1870–73)

Montaigne, Michel de. *The Diary of Montaigne's Journey to Italy*, trans. E. J. *Trenchman* (London: Hogarth Press, 1924), p. 12 for Jean le Bon's description of the bathhouse at Plombières.

Montaigne, Michel de. *The Complete Essays of Montaigne*, trans. Donald M. Frame (Stanford University Press, 1957), p. 318 for Frame's description of the effect of the 'Apology' as 'perplexing' in his headword to that chapter.

Montaigne, Michel de. *Oeuvres complètes*, ed. Albert Thibaudet and Maurice Rat (Paris: Gallimard, 1962)

Muchembled, Robert. *Culture Populaire et Culture des Élites dans la France Moderne* (Paris: Flammarion, 1978), p. 32 for the sad death of Jehann le Porcq.

Nietzsche, Friedrich. *Untimely Meditations*, trans. R. J. Hollingdale (Cambridge: Cambridge University Press, 1997), p. 135 for Nietzsche's approval of Montaigne.

Norton, Grace. 'The Use Made by Montaigne of Some Special Words', *Modern Language Notes*, 20 (1905), 243–8 for Montaigne's changes to words such as 'goust', 'noble' and 'monstrueux' over the various editions of his text.

Parker, Geoffrey. *The Military Revolution: Military Innovation and the Rise of the West, 1500–1800* (Cambridge: Cambridge University Press, 1996), p. 17 for the range and effectiveness of arquebuses; p. 60 for the youth and weakness of the men recruited to fire them.

Pegge, Samuel, *The Forme of Cury* (1780), pp. 161 for the medieval recipe for hippocras.

Popkin, Richard. *The History of Scepticism from Savonarola to Bayle* (Oxford: Oxford University Press, 2003)

Rawson, Claude. 'The Horror, the Holy Horror: Revulsion, Accusation and the Eucharist in the History of Cannibalism', *Times Literary Supplement*, 31 October 1997, 3–4 for links between Amerindian religion and Catholicism.

Reynolds, Edward. *A Treatise of the Passions and Faculties of the Soule of Man* (1647), p. 505 for Reynolds's scepticism about the linguistic capacities of animals.

Sayce, R. A. *The Essays of Montaigne: A Critical Exploration* (London: Weidenfeld and Nicolson, 1972)

Screech, M. A. *Montaigne's Annotated Copy of Lucretius: A Transcription and Study of the Manuscript, Notes and Pen-marks* (Geneva: Librairie Droz, 1998), p. 152 for Montaigne's annotations relating to taste; p. 499 for his erasing of Lucretius.

Starobinski, Jean. *Montaigne in Motion*, trans. Arthur Goldhammer (Chicago: Chicago University Press, 1985)

Stebbins, F. A. 'The Astronomical Instruments in Holbein's "Ambassadors"', *Journal of the Royal Astronomical Society of Canada*, 56 (1962), 45–52 for the astronomical instruments in the *Ambassadors*.

Supple, James. *Arms versus Letters: The Military and Literary Ideals in the Essays* (Oxford: Clarendon Press, 1984)

Tetsurō, Watsuji. *Rinrigaku: Ethics in Japan*, trans. Yamamoto Seisaku and Robert E. Carter (Albany: State University of New York Press, 1996)

Welles, Orson. *Interviews*, ed. Mark W. Estrin (Jackson: University Press of Mississippi, 2002), p. 62 for Welles's admiration of Montaigne.

Yuasa, Yasuo. *The Body: Toward an Eastern Mind–Body Theory*, ed. and trans. Thomas P. Kasulis and Shigenori Nagatomo (New York: State University of New York Press, 1987), p. 47 for Watsuji's view of the nature of friendship.

Illustrations

Index

Printed in the United States
by Baker & Taylor Publisher Services